DISCIPLESHIP

DISCIPLESHIP

WHAT IT TRULY MEANS TO BE A CHRISTIAN—
COLLECTED INSIGHTS FROM

A.W. TOZER

MOODY PUBLISHERS
CHICAGO

All Scripture quotations by A. W. Tozer, unless otherwise indicated, are taken from the King James Version.

All Scripture quotations in epigraphs, unless otherwise indicated, are taken from the Holy Bible, New International Version®, NIV®. Copyright © 1973, 1978, 1984, 2011 by Biblica, Inc.™ Used by permission of Zondervan. All rights reserved worldwide. www.zondervan.com. The "NIV" and "New International Version" are trademarks registered in the United States Patent and Trademark Office by Biblica, Inc.™

Edited by Kevin P. Emmert
Interior and Cover Design: Erik M. Peterson
Cover art by Aaron Joel Underwood (aaronjoelunderwood.com)

Library of Congress Cataloging-in-Publication Data

Names: Tozer, A. W. (Aiden Wilson), 1897-1963, author.
Title: Discipleship : what it truly means to be a Christian--collected
   insights / from A.W. Tozer.
Description: Chicago : Moody Publishers, 2018. | Includes bibliographical
   references.
Identifiers: LCCN 2018009883 (print) | LCCN 2018008663 (ebook) | ISBN
   9781600669019 (ebook) | ISBN 9781600668043
Subjects: LCSH: Christian life. | Spiritual life--Christianity.
Classification: LCC BV4501.3 (print) | LCC BV4501.3 .T7228 2018 (ebook) | DDC
   248.4--dc23
LC record available at https://lccn.loc.gov/2018009883

ISBN: 978-1-60066-804-3

We hope you enjoy this book from Moody Publishers. Our goal is to provide high-quality, thought-provoking books and products that connect truth to your real needs and challenges. For more information on other books and products written and produced from a biblical perspective, go to www.moodypublishers.com or write to:

Moody Publishers
820 N. LaSalle Boulevard
Chicago, IL 60610

1 3 5 7 9 10 8 6 4 2

Printed in the United States of America

CONTENTS

Publisher's Note 7

1. Marks of Discipleship 9

2. True and False Disciples 17

3. "Accepting" Christ 33

4. To All Who Received Him 49

5. Obedience Is Not an Option 61

6. You Cannot Face Two Directions 71

7. Crucified with Christ 81

8. Take Up Your Cross 99

9. Loving Righteousness, Hating Evil 105

10. Be Holy! 111

11. The Importance of Deeds 125

12. Preparing for Heaven 133

13. Go and Tell 143

References 149

PUBLISHER'S NOTE

What does it mean to be a disciple of Jesus Christ? At the most basic level, a disciple is a student, one who follows the teachings of a master and spreads those same teachings. Yet being a disciple of Christ is more than simply learning, adhering to, and spreading Christian doctrines. Being His disciple means being *His* follower, going wherever He leads and doing whatever He commands—no matter what the cost. A. W. Tozer knew this well.

What you hold in your hands is a collection of some of Tozer's most riveting writings on discipleship. These passages do not explore the *habits* of disciples—that is, prayer, Scripture reading, participation in worship services, fellowship with other believers, and so on—so much as the *marks* of true disciples. As you will soon discover, discipleship is not something we do, Tozer might say, but rather is a way of life. And being a disciple involves the total commitment of oneself to Jesus Himself. It cannot be done half-heartedly or part-time, and it certainly is not optional for those who profess Christ as Savior. In many ways, therefore, this volume explores what it means to be truly Christian.

Our hope is that, in reading this book, you will be stirred to follow Christ more ardently, to become like Him increasingly, and to glorify Him continually. May these words written by a mere man over half a century ago resonate with you today, challenging and encouraging you to give all you are to the God-man, Jesus Christ.

MARKS OF DISCIPLESHIP

Not everyone who says to me, "Lord, Lord,"
will enter the kingdom of heaven, but only the one
who does the will of my Father who is in heaven.

MATTHEW 7:21

In the New Testament salvation and discipleship are so closely related as to be indivisible. They are not identical, but as with Siamese twins they are joined by a tie which can be severed only at the price of death. Yet they *are* being severed in evangelical circles today. In the working creed of the average Christian salvation is held to be immediate and automatic, while discipleship is thought to be something optional that the Christian may delay indefinitely or never accept at all.

It is not uncommon to hear Christian workers urging seekers to accept Christ now and leave moral and social questions to be decided later. The notion is that obedience and discipleship are unrelated to salvation. We may be saved by believing a historic fact about Jesus Christ—that He died for our sins and rose again—and applying this to our personal situation. The whole biblical concept of lordship and obedience is completely absent from the mind of the seeker. He needs help, and Christ is the very one, even the only one, who can furnish it, so he "takes" Him as his personal Savior. The idea of His lordship is completely ignored.

The absence of the concept of discipleship from present-day Christianity leaves a vacuum that we instinctively try to fill with one or another substitute. I name a few.

SUBSTITUTES FOR DISCIPLESHIP

Pietism. By this I mean an enjoyable feeling of affection for the person of our Lord that is valued for itself and is wholly unrelated to cross-bearing or the keeping of the commandments of Christ. It is entirely possible to feel for Jesus an ardent love that is not of the Holy Spirit. Witness the love for the Virgin felt by certain devout souls, a love which in the very nature of things must be purely subjective. The heart is adept at emotional tricks and is entirely capable of falling in love with imaginary objects or romantic religious ideas.

In the confused world of romance, young persons are constantly inquiring how they can tell when they are "in love." They are afraid they may mistake some other sensation for true love and are seeking some trustworthy criterion by which they can judge the quality of their latest emotional fever. Their confusion of course arises from the erroneous notion that love is an enjoyable inward passion, without intellectual or volitional qualities and carrying with it no moral obligations.

Our Lord gave us a rule by which we can test our love for Him: "He that hath my commandments, and keepeth them, he it is that loveth me: and he that loveth me shall be loved of my Father, and I will love him, and will manifest myself to him. . . . If a man love me, he will keep my words. . . . He that loveth me not keepeth not my sayings" (John 14:21, 23–24).

These words are too plain to need much interpreting. Proof of love for Christ is simply removed altogether from the realm of the feelings and placed in the realm of practical obedience. I think the rest of the New Testament is in full accord with this.

Another substitute for discipleship is *literalism*. Our Lord referred to this when He reproached the Pharisees for their habit of tithing mint and anise and cumin while at the same time omitting the weightier matters of the Law such as justice, mercy and faith. Literalism manifests itself among us in many ways, but it can always be identified in that it lives by the letter of the Word while ignoring its spirit. It habitually fails to apprehend the inward meaning of Christ's words, and contents itself with external compliance with the text. If Christ commands baptism, for instance, it finds fulfillment in the act of water baptism, but the radical meaning of the act as explained in Romans 6 is completely overlooked. It reads the Scriptures regularly, contributes consistently to religious work, attends church every Sunday and otherwise carries on the common duties of a Christian; and for this it is to be commended. Its tragic breakdown is its failure to comprehend the lordship of Christ, the believer's discipleship, separation from the world and the crucifixion of the natural man.

Literalism attempts to build a holy temple upon the sandy foundation of the religious self. It will suffer, sacrifice and labor, but it will not die. It is Adam at his pious best, but it has never denied self to take up the cross and follow Christ.

Another substitute for discipleship I would mention (though these do not exhaust the list) is *zealous religious activity*. Working for Christ has today been accepted as the ultimate test of godliness among all but a few evangelical Christians. Christ has become a project to be promoted or a cause to be served instead of a Lord to be obeyed. Thousands of mistaken persons seek to do for Christ whatever their fancy suggests should be done, and in whatever way they think best. The what and the how of Christian service can only originate in the sovereign will of our Lord, but the busy beavers among us ignore this fact and think up their own schemes. The result is an army of men who run without being sent and speak without being commanded.

To avoid the snare of unauthorized substitution I recommend a careful and prayerful study of the lordship of Christ and the discipleship of the believer.

MARKS OF DISCIPLESHIP

The Christian Scriptures, particularly the gospel of John, contain two truths that appear to stand opposed to each other. One is that whosoever will may come to Christ. The other is that before anyone can come there must have been a previous work done in his heart by the sovereign operation of God.

The notion that just anybody, at any time, regardless of conditions, can start from religious scratch, without the Spirit's help, and believe savingly on Christ by a sudden decision of the will, is wholly contrary to the teachings of the Bible. God's invitation to men is broad but not unqualified. The word "whosoever" throws the door open wide, indeed, but the church in recent years has carried the gospel invitation far beyond its proper bounds and turned it into something more human and less divine than that found in the sacred Scriptures.

What we tend to overlook is that the word "whosoever" never stands by itself. Always its meaning is modified by the word "believe" or "will" or "come." According to the teachings of Christ no man will or can come and believe unless there has been done within him a prevenient work of God enabling him so to do.

In the sixth chapter of John our Lord makes some statements that gospel Christians seem afraid to talk about. The average one of us manages to live with them by the simple trick of ignoring them. They are such as these: (1) Only they come to Christ who have been given to Him by the Father (John 6:37). (2) No one can come of himself; he must first be drawn by the Father (John 6:44). (3) The ability to come to Christ is a gift of the Father (John 6:65). (4) Everyone given to the Son by the Father will come to Him (John 6:37).

It is not surprising that upon hearing these words many of our Lord's disciples went back and walked no more with Him. Such teaching cannot but be deeply disturbing to the natural mind. It takes from sinful men much of the power of self-determination upon which they had prided themselves so inordinately. It cuts the ground out from under their self-help and throws them back upon the sovereign good pleasure of God, and that is precisely where they do not want to be. They are willing to be saved by grace, but to preserve their self-esteem they must hold that the desire to be saved originated with them; this desire is their contribution to the whole thing, their offering of the fruit of the ground, and it keeps salvation in their hands where in truth it is not and can never be.

Admitting the difficulties this creates for us, and acknowledging that it runs contrary to the assumptions of popular Christianity, it is yet impossible to deny that there are certain persons who, though still unconverted, are nevertheless different from the crowd, marked out of God, stricken with an interior wound and susceptible to the call of Christ to a degree others are not.

About the teaching as a mere doctrine I am not much concerned, but I am keenly interested in learning how to identify such persons. No man is ever the same after God has laid His hand upon him. He will have certain marks, and though they are not easy to detect perhaps we may cautiously name a few.

One mark is *a deep reverence* for divine things. A sense of the sacred must be present or there can be no receptivity to God and truth. This mysterious feeling of awe precedes repentance and faith and is nothing else but a gift from heaven. Millions go through life unaffected by the presence of God in His world. Good they may be and honest, but they are nevertheless men of earth, "finished and finite clods," and proof against every call of the Spirit.

Another mark is *a great moral sensitivity.* Most persons are apathetic, insensitive to matters of the heart and the conscience, and so are not salvable, at least not in their present condition. But when God begins to work in a man to bring him to salvation He makes him acutely sensitive to evil. Inward repulsion toward the swine pen that rouses the prodigal and starts him back home is a gift of God to His chosen.

Another mark of the Spirit's working is *a mighty moral discontent*. In spite of our effort to make sinners think they are unhappy the fact is that wherever social and health conditions permit the masses of mankind enjoy themselves very much. Sin has its pleasures (Heb. 11:25) and the vast majority of human beings have a whale of a time living. The conscience is a bit of a pest but most persons manage to strike a truce with it quite early in life and are not troubled much by it thereafter.

It takes a work of God in a man to sour him on the world and to turn him against himself; yet until this has happened to him he is psychologically unable to repent and believe. Any degree of contentment with the world's moral standards or his own lack of holiness successfully blocks off the flow of faith into the man's heart. Esau's fatal flaw was moral complacency; Jacob's only virtue was his bitter discontent.

Again before a man can be saved he must feel *a consuming spiritual hunger*. Anyone who lives close to the hearts of men knows that there is little spiritual hunger among them. Religion, pious talk, yes; but not real hunger. Where a hungry heart is found we may be sure that God was there first. "Ye have not chosen me, but I have chosen you" (John 15:16).

TRUE AND FALSE DISCIPLES

If you hold to my teaching, you are really my disciples. Then you will know the truth, and the truth will set you free.

JOHN 8:31–32

We can learn quite a bit from what is *not* said or written. For example, if I say "up," I imply that there must be a "down." If I say "long," I imply also a "short," or I would not have had to say "long." If I say "good," there must be a "bad," else there would be nothing to compare "good" with. So when Jesus spoke of real disciples, there must have been other kinds as well.

Before we consider some of the other kinds of disciples, as compared with "real" disciples, notice the framework of Jesus' discussion with the Pharisees. First, they had asked Him, "Where is thy Father?" (John 8:19). And Jesus had dared to reply, "Ye neither know me, nor my Father: if ye had known me, ye should have known my Father also" (8:19). Then He continued, "I go my way, and ye shall seek me, and shall die in your sins: whither I go, ye cannot come" (8:21).

A bit later, they asked the impudent question, "Who art thou?" (8:25). Jesus replied in effect, "I am the One I have been telling you I am. Did I not say, 'Destroy this temple, and in three days I will raise it up' (John 2:19)? That is who I am! I referred to Myself and said, 'The Son of Man is in heaven.' (See Matt. 26:64.) That is who I am. I said, 'I that speak unto thee am he [the Christ]' (John 4:26). I said, 'The Son quickeneth whom he will' (John 5:21)—that is who I am.

"I said, 'I am the living bread which came down from heaven: if any man eat of this bread, he shall live for ever' (John 6:51). I said, 'I am the light of the world. Whoever follows me will never walk in darkness.' That also is who I am. I speak and I judge, and the Father is with me because I do always what pleases the Father. I am the Spokesperson from the Father. That is who I am!"

JESUS WAS GOD SPEAKING

Do not fail to notice that Jesus could and did say, "I speak and I judge. I speak from the Father." Jesus was not in the business of offering human advice that people could take or leave as they wished. Instead, He always spoke with absolute, final authority. He was not just a man speaking. His was not just advice from a good, religious man. He was God speaking. This, then, was what Jesus told His questioners:

I am from above. . . . But he that sent me is true; and I speak to the world those things which I have heard of him. . . .

I do nothing of myself; but as my Father hath taught me, I speak these things. . . . The Father hath not left me alone. (John 8:23, 26, 28–29)

Jesus was declaring that He spoke for the Father, from whose absolute message there was no appeal. This was quite different from what we hear about in ecclesiastical circles today. A bishop says, "It is to be like this. . . ." However, his decree can always be appealed to the archbishop. But when the Lord Jesus Christ speaks, there is no appeal. It is either Jesus or everlasting night. It is either listen to what He says or be forever in ignorance. It is either take His light, or be forever in darkness.

Immediately, someone is bound to protest. "What arrogance! What intolerance! I do not believe Christians should be intolerant!" Well, I can startle such a person a little more. I believe in Christian charity, but I do not believe at all in Christian tolerance. The person who hates the name of Jesus, who believes that He was not the Son of God but an imposter, deserves charity on our part. I think if I lived next door to such a person, I would not put a fence between us. If I worked with him or her, I would not refuse to be friendly. I believe in Christian charity, but I do not believe in the weak tolerance that we hear preached so often now—the idea that Jesus must tolerate everyone and that the Christian must tolerate every kind of doctrine. I do not believe it for one minute, for there are not a dozen "rights." There is only one "right." There is but one Jesus and one God and one Bible.

When we become so tolerant that we lead people into mental fog and spiritual darkness, we are not acting like Christians. We are acting like cowards! We cannot do better than to remember that when Jesus Christ has spoken, that is it!

When Jesus claimed to have come from the heart of the Father, when He was declared to be the eternal Word who was in the beginning with God, who was and is God, we are hearing truth. Our position is clear. It is not Jesus plus a number of other philosophies. It is Jesus only. He is enough. . . .

An honest person may come to Jesus seeking, yet not understanding. It may take a week or a month, a year or ten years to help him or her understand. But that person can be sure of this: our Lord will never, never say anything but what He has said. Never will He hedge. Never will He put in a footnote, "I didn't quite mean it like that." He said what He meant. He meant what He said. He is the Eternal Word, and we must listen to Him if our discipleship is to be genuine and consistent.

We ought to think with joy about those who are true disciples of Jesus Christ. A true disciple has not taken an impulsive leap in the dark. That person is one who has become a Christian after deep thought and proper consideration. A true disciple has allowed the Word of God to search his or her heart. A true disciple has felt the sense of personal sin and the need to be released from it. A true disciple has come to believe that Jesus Christ is the only person who can release him or her from guilt. A true disciple has committed himself or herself without equivocation, without reservation to Jesus Christ the Savior.

A true disciple does not consider Christianity a part-time commitment. That person has become a Christian in all departments of his or her life. A true disciple has reached the point in Christian experience where there is no turning back. Follow him or her for 24 hours of the day and night. You will find you can count on that person's faithfulness to Christ and his or her joyful abiding in the Word of God.

FALSE DISCIPLES

Now, what about the other kinds of disciples?

First, we must consider the person who becomes a disciple of Christ on impulse. This is likely to be the person who came in on a wave of enthusiasm, and I am a little bit suspicious of anyone who is too easily converted. I have a feeling that if he or she can be easily converted to Christ, he or she may be very easily flipped back the other way. I am concerned about the person who just yields, who has no sales resistance at all.

I like the sinner who means business, even though at first he or she may be standing up, looking you right in the eye, and saying, "I don't believe it and I won't do it!" The time will come when that person will think better of it. He or she will take time to cool off, will take time to listen to and meditate on the Word. Slowly but surely, he or she will determine that the way of Christ is the right way. When that person becomes a Christian, you have got somebody!

But the one who is a "flip-flopper," easy to push around, will be easily pushed out again. If he or she can be reasoned into the kingdom, he or she can be scared out again in no time.

Some have become disciples because they found themselves in just the right frame of mind. Here is a man whose mother died recently. The invitation song is "Tell Mother I'll Be There," and he comes forward weeping. People think he is a penitent man, but in reality he is only thinking about his mother. Christianity on impulse is not the answer to discipleship. God will not stampede us into the kingdom of God. The Bible is true when it declares, "Now is the accepted time; behold, now is the day of salvation" (2 Cor. 6:2), but God does not want people to be helped from their cocoons before they are ready.

Actually, I go along with the man or woman who is thoughtful enough about this decision to say truthfully: "I want a day to think this over," or, "I want a week to read the Bible and to meditate on what this decision means."

I have never considered it a very great compliment to the Christian church that we can generate enthusiasm on such short notice. The less there is in the kettle, the quicker it begins to boil. There are some who get converted on enthusiasm and backslide on principle!

PERSONALITY-ENAMORED DISCIPLES

I have also met the kind of disciples who seemed to be Christians because of the cult of personality. They had been overwhelmed and charmed by a big dose of winsome personality. You cannot deny that when some people flash their broad smiles, their faces radiate charm and people want to follow them immediately.

I have always been bothered a little by personality tests, even though I am addicted to them. Actually, I have never found one that really benefited me. I always seem to come out with a poor score. But I never pass one up if it asks, "Are you a good husband?" "Are you a good father?" "Have you got personality?"

I once confided to Dr. H. M. Shuman, long-time president of

The Christian and Missionary Alliance and a very wise Christian philosopher, "Dr. Shuman, no one will follow me. I can't help but notice all of the big leaders with their charm and personality to spare. All they have to do is whistle, and there come the crowds!"

"Just thank God that they are not following you," Dr. Shuman replied. "Although they may not follow you, preach Jesus and they will follow *Him*!"

When you think about it, we are told that Jesus Himself had no beauty that we should desire Him (Isa. 53:2). He was not a personality boy. I think He must have been a plain-looking Jew, for Judas had to kiss Him to let the soldiers know which one He was. If Jesus had been a television personality and had looked the part, no one would have had to go up and spot Him.

But when Jesus opened His mouth, grace and truth came out, and men and women either rejected the words that fell from His lips or they followed Him. In either case, they could never be the same again.

HALF-DISCIPLES

Now, think with me about those who are demi-disciples—that is, part-disciples, half-disciples. These are men and women who bring their lives partially under the control of Christ, but they leave whole other areas outside His control. Long ago I came to the conclusion that if Jesus Christ is not controlling all of me, the chances are very good that He is not controlling any of me.

It may sound strange, but I have met Christian disciples who were half-saved. Please do not ask me to identify them theologically. I cannot. I am glad that God does not ask me to write letters of recommendation for some people whom He cannot place! He is not asking me that, for He knows where everyone is—in or out of the kingdom—and I do not.

I only know this about some of these people whom I see as half-disciples: they will allow the Lord to bother them on some things, but certainly not on others. They will obey the Lord in select areas of their lives but disobey Him willfully in others. The result is I do not know where to put them. I do not know what to do with them. Therefore, I must leave them with God.

As for myself, I do not want to be a half-disciple. I want my whole life—all of me—under the dominion of the Lord Jesus Christ. It was an old English preacher who used to say, "If Christ cannot be Lord of all, He will not be Lord at all!" Certainly, He wants to be Lord of all of my life. He wants me to be a disciple who will allow Him to rule my entire being.

Suppose a young Christian man starts out with a shining face. He kneels at the prayer meeting and says, "Lord, take me and use me!" He seems to be an exemplary, consecrated Christian man. Then a beautiful girl comes along. She is not a Christian, but she is nice to look at and she has a winsome personality and a soft voice. The young man becomes interested in her, and she starts to lead him away. Eventually, there is a wedding, and they get their home set up, and soon the young man is among those who do not show up for prayer meeting. You ask him about it, and he replies, "Well, my wife had another plan for me." Before long, he is a part-Christian and part-husband, not working very hard at either one.

I do not want to be cruel, but I must be honest: Jesus Christ wants to be and must be Lord. He must be head of and Lord of all departments of our lives. We cannot have a girlfriend or a husband or a home or a job shut up in an airtight compartment that Jesus cannot control. If Jesus is not Lord of all of us, we are not real disciples.

SHORT-TERM DISCIPLES

Others are disciples—but only for the short term. I have met some of them. They always leave a way out. They never burn their bridges behind them. They never reach the point of no return. I believe a Christian is a Christian indeed, a real disciple, when he or she has reached the point of no return.

The people in our churches would not be worrying so much about whether they can or cannot be lost after they are saved if they would just come right down to business with God. They need to say, "Lord, I am not going to worry about such theological problems. I am going to face it now, and reach the point of no return. I will not be going back." But there still are short-term disciples who have not yet reached that point. They are part-time, short-term. They are seasonal disciples. They come to church on Easter Sunday, at Christmas and at other special times. They can be very religious in certain seasons.

CHAMELEON DISCIPLES

Have you ever heard of "chameleon" disciples? They can change color with the environment. There are even some preachers like that. They can talk the language of the crowd they happen to be with. If they are with liberal thinkers, behold, they begin to sound liberal. If they were with evangelicals, they sound evangelical. They are "adaptable," they say. "We believe in adjustment." They do not need adjustment; they need God!

As Christian disciples, we should be whatever we are wherever we are. Like diamonds. A diamond does not adjust; it is always a diamond. Just so, Christians ought always to be Christians. We are not Christians if we have to wait for the right atmosphere to practice our religion. We are not Christians if we have to go to church to be blessed. We are not Christians until we are thoroughly Christ's—until we have reached the point of no return, not seasonal anymore, but regular always. Then, the Lord says, we are real disciples. We are following on to know the Lord!

It may be well to look at some of the marks of those who are not really disciples. Some of them have a pious look. In fact, on Sunday mornings, they look as pious as stuffed owls. We have some of them in our evangelical circles. People can afford to be pious at 10:45 a.m. on Sundays. It is a most convenient hour. They do not have to be religious to get up in time for 10:45 a.m. church. They do not lose out on their Sunday dinners, either. They get a little fresh air. The service does not last long. The music is good most of the time. It only costs them the dollar they drop in the offering plate.

So, those who go to church only once a week—on Sunday morning—leave themselves wide open to the suspicion that they are only part-time, Sunday-morning disciples. They are not in church enough to prove that they are any other kind of disciple.

DISCIPLES WITH MULTIPLE LOVES

Another mark is this: they have not given up their other loves. Fénelon, many years ago, said, "Give up thy loves in order that thou mightest find *the* love. Give up thy lovers that thou mightest find the great *Lover*. Give up all that thou lovest in order that thou mightest find the *One* whom thou canst love." But these "other" disciples will not do that—they will not give up their other loves. They want to take the world in one hand and the cross in the other and walk the tightrope between heaven and hell. They hope by the grace of God to make one last final jump over the portals.

No, I think not. I remember Balaam in the Scriptures. He prayed a plaintive prayer, and on the strength of that prayer, half the preachers in this country would have drummed him straight into heaven. He said, "Let me die the death of the righteous, and let my last end be like his!" (Num. 23:10). But then he went over to the side of the sinners and fought against the righteous in battle. When he died, what kind of death did he die? Did he die the death of the righteous? I say no. He died the death of the sinner because he had lived the life of a sinner. The person who wants to die the death of the righteous must live the life of the righteous. The person who wants to die a Christian must live a Christian. The person who wants the Advocate above to be a shelter for him or her in that hour must allow Him to be a shelter right now!

OTHER MARKS

Do you want to know another mark of the "other" disciples? Well, they will always be attracted to their own crowd. They will always go their own company. In most churches, there are some who claim to be disciples who have scarcely attended a prayer meeting a year. Some time ago Dr. William Pettengil spelled it out for us. He was preaching from the Acts, and he came to the passage, "And being let go, [Peter and John] went to their own company" (4:23). Dr. Pettengil bore down rather hard on the fact that all of us human beings, if free to do so, generally gravitate to our own company. Let some people go, and they will soon be fishing with other fishermen. Let another group go, and before long they will be in a music hall listening to an opera. Let others go and you will soon find them sitting at the race track watching the horses. Christians flock together, too. Those who have a prayer meeting heart will be at the prayer meeting. If we have Christian hearts, we will be more than Sunday morning Christians.

There are also those who say, "I am a disciple of Christ," but they flippantly ignore—or reject—many of His words and commandments.

Some teachers have tried to enshroud Jesus in a pink fog of sentimentality. But there is really no excuse for misunderstanding Him. He drew the line as taut as a violin string. He said, "He that is not with me is against me; and he that gathereth not with me scattereth abroad" (Matt. 12:30). "But he that believeth not is condemned already, because he hath not believed in the name of the only begotten Son of God" (John 3:18). "And he that believeth not the Son shall not see life; but the wrath of God abideth on him" (John 3:36). At that great day when He judges mankind, Jesus says He "shall separate them one from another, as a shepherd divideth his sheep from the goats." The one group "shall go away into everlasting punishment: but the righteous into life eternal" (Matt. 25:32, 46). Those statements leave no twilight zone, no in-between.

TRUE DISCIPLES

Consider the benefits promised to the true disciples. Jesus said, "And ye shall know the truth, and the truth shall make you free" (John 8:32). No one can know truth except the one who obeys truth. You think you know truth. People memorize the Scriptures by the yard, but that is not a guarantee of knowing the truth. Truth is not a text. Truth is in the text, but it takes the text plus the Holy Spirit to bring truth to a human soul. A person can memorize a text, but the truth must come from the Holy Spirit through the text. Faith comes by hearing the Word, but faith is also the gift of God by the Holy Spirit.

Truth must be understood by inward illumination. Then we know the truth. Until that time, we do not know it. That is why Jesus said, "If ye continue in my word"—that is, if you continue in My teachings—"then are ye my disciples indeed; and ye shall know the truth, and the truth shall make you free" (John 8:31–32).

I heard through missionaries of a boy overseas who had memorized Jesus' entire Sermon on the Mount. He did it in such record time and with such apparently little effort that someone called him in to find out how he had done it. "Well," said the boy, "I would memorize a verse and then trust God to help me put it into practice. Then I would memorize the next verse and say, 'Lord, help me to live this one, too.'" The boy said that in that fashion he had memorized the entire Sermon on the Mount.

That boy had truth on his side. He did not consider truth to be something objective, simply to be filed in the mind as knowledge. Rather, truth to him was also subjective—to be acted on. Truth becomes real to us within our beings by obedience and faith.

Charles G. Finney taught that it was wrong—morally wrong—to teach objective doctrine without a moral application. I have gone to Bible classes and listened to men who were learned in the Word of God. Still I have come away as cold as a pickled fish. There was no help, no lift in my spirit, nothing to warm the inside of my heart. The truth had been given to me just like a proposition in Euclid or a mathematical formula from Pythagoras. And the answer is, "So what? Let's go and have a soda!" Are we aware that we can give people objective truth without moral application? If God's moral Word is true, it means us. And if it means us, we ought to obey it. That is life. That is knowing the truth.

Not only can we know truth, but the truth makes us free. How we long for that benefit! There is a doxology to Jesus in the Revelation that reads like this:

Unto him that loved us, and *washed* us from our sins in his own blood, And hath made us kings and priests unto God and his Father; to him be glory and dominion for ever and ever. Amen. (Rev. 1:5–6, emphasis added)

Notice the word *washed*. What does a laundry do with our clothes? Our contacts with civilization make our clothes dirty, greasy, sometimes spotted. The dirt is not only on our clothes; soon it is actually *in* them. We can shake the garment, argue with it, talk to it, read Shakespeare to it, lecture it on patriotism or the advances of civilization. Still it is soiled and dirty. The dirt must be loosed. The garment must be set free from its soil.

At the laundry the garment is immersed in a solution that looses the dirt. Then it is rinsed, dried, pressed and sent back to its wearer, clean and presentable. But it had to undergo a process that would free it from the dirt.

The only solution that will loose us from our sins is the blood of Jesus Christ. He loved us and freed us—washed us—from our sins in His own blood. Education, refinement—nothing else worked. But when Jesus' blood did its work, we were free! "And ye shall know the truth," Jesus said, "and the truth shall make you free" (John 8:32). The truth will lead you to the cross, to the Lamb, to the fountain filled with blood, and you will be free from your sins. But there must be a moral commitment. If there is not, there is no understanding. If there is no understanding, there is no cleansing.

Are you obeying the truth as it is revealed by the Spirit of God? Are you enjoying the benefits of freedom in Jesus Christ? Are you one of His *true* disciples?

"ACCEPTING" CHRIST

*The Son of Man must be lifted up, that everyone
who believes may have eternal life in him.*

JOHN 3:14–15

Some things in our human lives are so basically unimportant that we never miss them if we do not have them. Some other things, even some that we just take for granted, are so important that if we do not grasp them and hold them and secure them for all eternity, we will suffer irreparable loss and anguish. When we come to the question of our own relationship with God through the merits of our Lord Jesus Christ, we come to one of those areas that in a supreme degree is truly a matter of life and death.

This is so desperately a matter of importance for every human being who comes into the world that I first become indignant, and then I become sad, when I try to give spiritual counsel to a person who looks me in the eye and tells me, "Well, I am trying to make up my mind if I should accept Christ or not." Such a person gives absolutely no indication that he realizes he is talking about the most important decision he can make in his lifetime—a decision to get right with God, to believe in the eternal Son, the Savior, to become a disciple, an obedient witness to Jesus Christ as Lord.

How can any man or woman, lost and undone, sinful and wretched, alienated from God, stand there and intimate that the death and resurrection of Jesus Christ and God's revealed plan of salvation do not take priority over some of life's other decisions?

Now, the particular attitude revealed here about "accepting Christ" is wrong because it makes Christ stand hat-in-hand, somewhere outside the door, waiting on our human judgment. We know about His divine person, we know that He is the Lamb of God who suffered and died in our place. We know all about His credentials. Yet we let Him stand outside on the steps like some poor timid fellow who is hoping he can find a job. We look Him over, then read a few more devotional verses, and ask: "What do you think, Mabel? Do you think we ought to accept Him? I really wonder if we should accept Him." And so, in this view, our poor Lord Christ stands hat-in-hand, shifting from one foot to another looking for a job, wondering whether He will be accepted. Meanwhile, there sits the proud Adamic sinner, rotten as the devil and filled with all manner of spiritual leprosy and cancer. But he is hesitating; he is judging whether or not he will accept Christ.

PUTTING OFF THE CHRIST

Doesn't that proud human know that the Christ he is putting off is the Christ of God, the eternal Son who holds the worlds in His hands? Does he not know that Christ is the eternal Word, the Jesus who made the heavens and the earth and all things that are therein? Why, this One who patiently waits for our human judgment is the One who holds the stars in His hands. He is the Savior and Lord and head over all things to the church. It will be at His word that the graves shall give up their dead, and the dead shall come forth, alive forevermore. At His word, the fire shall burst loose and burn up the earth and the heavens and the stars and planets shall be swept away like a garment.

He is the One, the Mighty One! And yet there He stands, while we animated clothespins—that's what we look like and that's what we are—decide whether we will accept Him or not. How grotesque can it be? The question ought not to be whether I will accept Him; the question ought to be whether He will accept me! But He does not make that a question. He has already told us that we do not have to worry or disturb our minds about that. "And him that cometh to me I will in no wise cast out" (John 6:37). He has promised to receive us, poor and sinful though we be. But the idea that we can make Him stand while we render the verdict of whether He is worthy of our acceptance is a frightful calumny—and we ought to get rid of it!

Now, I think we should get back to our original premise that our relationship to Jesus Christ is a matter of life or death to us. The average person with even a minimum of instruction in church or Sunday school will generally take two things for granted, without argument. The first is that Jesus Christ came into the world to save sinners. That is declared specifically in the Bible, and it is declared in other words adding up to the same thing all through the New Testament. If we have been reared in gospel churches, we also generally will take for granted the second fact: that we are saved by faith in Christ alone, without our works and without our merit.

I am discussing these two basic things with you here because too many individuals take them for granted, believe them to be true; and still they are asking, "How do I know that I have come into a saving relationship with Jesus Christ?" We had better find the answer because this is the matter of life or death.

The fact that Christ Jesus came into the world to save sinners is a matter of record. It needs no further proof. It is a fact— yet the world is not saved! Right here in America, in our own neighborhoods, thousands and tens of thousands of people still are not saved. Just the fact that He came to save sinners is not enough—that fact in itself cannot save us. A friend or neighbor may tell us, "Well, I have gone to this certain church all my life. I have been confirmed, baptized and all the rest. I am going to take the chance that it will get me through."

My friend, your odds are not that good—you do not even have a chance. If your relation to Jesus Christ is not a saving relation, then you are on your own without a guide and without a compass. It is not a chance you have; it is suicide that you are committing. It is not a chance in ten times ten thousand. It is either be right or be dead; in this case, be right or be eternally lost.

There are millions all around us who have some Bible knowledge. They would tell you they have no argument with the fact that Jesus Christ came into the world to save sinners. They may even make a little joke about their own failures and shortcomings—they would not call them sins. They would likely excuse themselves from having to make a personal decision because they are not nearly as bad as Mr. Jones or Mrs. Smith down the street.

The point is that they may be able to recite John 3:16 or quote something nice about the whole world needing a Savior—and in an unusually tender moment there might be the sign of a tear in the eye. But they are lost. They are really far from God. They know that they are not converted because they have all known some person who had confessed Jesus Christ, been soundly converted and started living a transformed life.

Yes, they all know the difference. They know they are not converted, but they would rather not be told about the fate of the sinner when he dies. Oh, that lost men and women would get concerned to the point of asking and finding out how they may come into a saving relationship with the Savior, Jesus Christ!

THREE ANSWERS

Now, go to the average Christian brother, a converted man and probably a substitute teacher for the Bible class, and ask him: "How can I come into a saving relation to Jesus Christ so that it works for me?" He will probably give you one of three answers, or he may give you all three answers. If you came to me, you would get the same, so this is not a criticism of anyone. This is simply a statement. You would get the same answer from Billy Graham and you would get the same answer from the most isolated and unknown layman who has committed his way to Jesus Christ.

First, you would be told that it is a matter of faith, that you must believe what God says about His Son, as in Acts 16:31: "Believe on the Lord Jesus Christ, and thou shalt be saved." That is the Bible answer that you would get.

Then, the person answering your question might add: "There

is also the willingness to receive from God, as in John 1:12: 'But as many as received him . . . even to them that believe on his name.'" So there in John's gospel, you find the close relationship in faith of believing and receiving.

But in our day, you will also be likely to get a third answer, and that is the one we are considering here. In all likelihood, if you would ask a number of Christian people how to come into this blessed saving relationship with Christ, someone is going to tell you: "Why, you just accept Christ!"

Let me say here that I do not want to make God responsible for anything I do, or anything I tell you. I have had my long talks with God and He knows how grateful and thankful I am if He can bless me and guide me and use me to do a few little things for Him. He surely knows that I am available as long as I am able to pray and think and speak a good word for Him, as long as I last.

What I am saying on this contemporary subject of "accepting Christ" is not a personal whim. Actually, I was kneeling by the little couch in my study upstairs, kneeling there with my Bible open, and I was engaged with God in doing a little repenting on my own accord—my own.

All of this came to me so clearly that I just wrote down a few notes, and said, "I am going to talk to the people about this." You are my friends, and I tell you that perhaps I am introducing some things here that God did not say to me, but maybe you will agree that you would rather hear a sermon from the outline the man got while on his knees than to know that he had gotten it somewhere else.

Well, that is it; a popular answer in our day is that we find

Christ by accepting Him. You will find when I am through that I am not being critical. Probably our expressions in language do not always tell us what our hearts know.

NOT FOUND IN THE BIBLE

You may be surprised, as I was, when I ran this thing down and found that the expression "accept Christ" does not occur in the Bible. It is not found in the New Testament at all. I have looked it up in *Strong's Exhaustive Concordance*, and the old editors worked on that volume so long and so thoroughly that it does not skip a single word. Strong's concordance shows very definitely that the word accept is never used in the Bible in the sense of our accepting God or accepting Jesus as our Savior. It does seem strange that while we do not find its use anywhere in the Bible, the phrase, "Will you accept Christ?" or "Have you accepted Christ?" have become the catchwords throughout our soul-winning circles. I am not trying to question our good intentions. I am sure that I have used this same expression many times—but still we have to admit that it does not occur in the Bible at all.

The words *accept* and *acceptance* are used in the Scriptures in a number of ways, but never in connection with believing on Christ or receiving Christ for salvation or being saved. My concern in this matter is my feeling that "easy acceptance" has been fatal to millions of people who may have stopped short in matters of faith and obedience.

It is interesting to note that many groups of Christian workers and preachers and evangelists everywhere are calling for revival. Spiritual life in many areas seems to be in a low state and in many cases people are passing along the word about "prayer for revival." But here is the odd thing: no one seems to stop and raise a question, such as: "Perhaps the reason we need revival so badly is the fact that we did not get started right in the first place." This is why I have questioned the wide use of the soul-winning catchword, "Will you accept Christ? Just bow your head and accept Christ!"

I cannot estimate the number, although I think it is a very large number, of people who have been brought into some kind of religious experience by a fleeting formality of "accepting Christ," and a great, great number of them are still not saved. They have not been brought into a genuine saving relationship with Jesus Christ. We see the results all around us—they generally behave like religious sinners instead of like born-again believers.

That is why there is such a great stirring about the need for revival. That is why so many are asking, "What is the matter with us? We seem so dead, so lifeless, so apathetic about spiritual things!"

I say again that I have come to the conclusion that there are far too many among us who have thought that they accepted Christ—but nothing has come of it within their own lives and desires and habits. Will you just examine this matter a little more closely with me?

This kind of philosophy in soul winning, the idea that it is the easiest thing in the world to "accept Jesus," permits the man or woman to accept Christ by an impulse of the mind, or emotions. It allows us to gulp twice and sense an emotional feeling that may come over us, and then say, "I have accepted Christ."

All of you are aware of some of the very evident examples of the shortcomings in this approach to conversion and the new birth. A Christian lady interested in the boys and girls goes out to the playground where several hundred children are engaged in their play and games. When she comes back, she reports with enthusiasm that she was able to persuade a group of about seventy children to stop their play and "accept Christ in their hearts."

AN ILLUSTRATION

I actually was told of a group of preachers and laymen gathered in a hotel dining room and when the issue of soul-winning came up, one of the preachers said, "It is the easiest thing in the world, and I will give you a demonstration."

When the waiter came to his table, this brother said, "Can I have a minute of your time?"

The waiter said, "Yes, sir."

"Are you a Christian?" the preacher asked.

"No, sir. I am not a Christian."

"Wouldn't you like to be a Christian?"

"Well—well, I haven't thought too much about it."

"You know, all you have to do is accept Christ into your heart—will you accept Him?"

"Well, I guess so—yes, sir."

"All right, then, you just bow your head for a moment."

So, while the man who has been placed in a corner is thinking most about his tip, the soul-winner prays: "Now, Lord, here is a man who wants to accept You. And he takes You now as his Savior. Bless him real good. Amen!"

So, the waiter gets an enthusiastic handshake, and turns

away to do his job, and he is just the same as when he came into the room.

But the demonstrating preacher turns to the group and says, "It is a simple matter. You can all see how easy it is to lead someone to Christ."

I think these are matters about which we must be legitimately honest and in which we must seek the discernment of the Holy Spirit. I hope that the waiter had better sense than the reverend because if he did not he is damned. These are things about which we cannot afford to be wrong. To be wrong is to still be lost and far from God. This is a matter of life or death and eternity. When we are considering the importance to any human being of a right and saving relationship to Jesus Christ, we cannot afford to be wrong.

I think there is much abuse and that it is a great misconception to try to deal with men and women in this shallow manner when we know the great importance of conviction and concern and repentance when it comes to conversion, spiritual regeneration, being born from above by the Spirit of God. It would be a healthy sign if the whole church of Christ would rise up and ask God for fresh air in this matter; asking God for courage to consider and analyze where we stand in our efforts to win people to the Savior.

I am not trying to downgrade anybody in his or her efforts to win souls. I am just of the opinion that we are often too casual and there are too many tricks that can be used to make soul-winning encounters completely painless and at no cost and with no inconvenience.

Some people that we deal with on this "quick and easy" basis have such little preparation and are so ignorant of the plan of salvation that they would be willing to bow their heads and "accept" Buddha or Zoroaster or Father Divine if they thought that they could get rid of us in that way.

AN OLD TESTAMENT ILLUSTRATION

I think back to that time when God was dealing with the Israelites in bondage in Egypt. Suppose that Moses had said to the Israelites, "Do you accept the blood on the doorpost?"

They would have said, "Yes, of course. We accept the blood."

Moses then would have said, "That's fine. Now goodbye; I will be seeing you."

They would have stayed right in Egypt, slaves for the rest of their lives. But their acceptance of the blood was a decision of action. Their acceptance of the blood of the Passover meant that they stayed awake all night; girded, ready, shoes on their feet, staffs in their hands, eating the food of the Passover, ready for the moving of God. Then, when the trumpet blasts sang sweet and clear, they all arose and started for the Red Sea. When they got to the Red Sea, having acted in faith, God was there to hold back the sea and they went out, never to return! Their acceptance had the right kind of feet under it. Their acceptance gave them the guts to do something about it in the demonstration of their faith in God and His word.

Consider also the case of the prodigal son in the midst of the pigs with their dirt and filth and smell. Suppose you were concerned about him, about his own rags and his hunger.

"I have good news for you," you tell him. "Your father will

forgive you if you will accept it. Will you accept it?"

He looks up from where he is reclining among the pigs, trying to keep warm, and replies: "Yeah, I'll accept it."

"Do you accept your father's reconciling and saving word?"

"Yes, I do!"

"That's fine. All right, goodbye. Hope to see you again."

You leave him in the pigpen. You leave him still in the dirt and filth. But that is not the way it happened in the story Jesus told in Luke 15.

The fellow was in there with the pigs and the filth—but something was stirring in his own heart and mind, and he said within himself: "If I am ever going to get out of this mess, I will have to make a decision. I must arise and go to my father."

I guess all of us know the next line:

"So he got up and went!"

Remember that?

"So he got up and went!"

Acceptance to the Jews meant strict obedience from that moment on. Acceptance to the prodigal son meant repentance in line with his acceptance.

I realize that the word *accept* has come close to being a synonym for the word receive. But I want to tell you what it means to accept Christ and then I want you to search your own heart and say, "Have I ever really accepted Christ? Do I accept Christ? Have I accepted Him at all?"

I want to give you a definition for accepting Christ. *To accept Christ in anything like a saving relation is to have an attachment to the person of Christ that is revolutionary, complete, and exclusive.* What I am talking about is an attachment to the person of

Christ, and that is so important. It is something more than getting in with a crowd that you like. It is something more than the social fellowship of some nice fellow that gives you a thrill when you touch his hand. It is something more than getting in with a group that puts on their uniforms and plays softball together on Tuesday evenings.

Those things are all harmless enough, God knows. But accepting Jesus Christ is more than finding association with a group you like. It is not just going on a picnic or taking a hike. We have those activities in our church and I believe in them. But they are not the things that are as important as your acceptance of Jesus Christ. The answer you are seeking in Jesus Christ does not mean that you are just getting in with a religious group who may not be any better off than you are.

Accepting Jesus Christ, receiving Jesus Christ into your life means that you have made an attachment to the person of Christ that is revolutionary in that it reverses the life and transforms it completely. It is an attachment to the person of Christ. It is complete in that it leaves no part of the life unaffected. It exempts no area of the life of the total man; his total being.

This kind of an attachment to the person of Christ means that Christ is not just one of several interests. It means that He is the one exclusive attachment as the sun is the exclusive attachment of the earth. As the earth revolves around the sun, and the sun is its center and the core of its being, so Jesus Christ is the Son of righteousness, and to become a Christian by the grace of God means to come into His orbit and begin to revolve around Him exclusively.

In the sense of spiritual life and desire and devotion, it means to revolve around Him completely, exclusively—not partly around Him.

This does not mean that we do not have other relationships— we all do because we all live in a complex world. You give your heart to Jesus. He becomes the center of your transformed life. But you may be a man with a family. You are a citizen of the country. You have a job and an employer. In the very nature of things, you have other relationships. But by faith and through grace, you have now formed an exclusive relationship with your Savior, Jesus Christ. All of your other relationships are now conditioned and determined by your one relationship to Jesus Christ, the Lord.

Jesus laid down the terms of Christian discipleship and there have been people who have criticized and said, "Those words of Jesus sound harsh and cruel." His words were plain and He was saying to every one of us: "If you have other relationships in life which are more important and more exclusive than your spiritual relationship to the eternal Savior, then you are not My disciple."

FIRST AND LAST AND ALL

To accept Christ, then, is to attach ourselves to His holy person; to live or die, forever. He must be first and last and all. All of our other relationships are conditioned and determined and colored by our one exclusive relation to Him. To accept Christ without reservation is to accept His friends as your friends from that moment on.

If you find yourself in an area where Christ has no friends, you will be friendless except for the one Friend who sticketh closer than a brother. It means that you will not compromise your life. You will neither compromise your talk nor your habits of life.

We have to confess that we find there are people who are such cowards that when they are with a crowd that denies the Son of God and disgraces the holy name of Jesus, they allow themselves to be carried away in that direction. Are they Christians? You will have to answer that.

A Christian is one who has accepted Jesus' friends as his friends and Jesus' enemies as his enemies by an exclusive attachment to the person of Christ.

I made up my mind a long time ago. Those who declare themselves enemies of Jesus Christ must look upon me as their enemy—and I ask no quarter from them. And if they are the friends of Jesus Christ they are my friends and I do not care what color they are or what denomination they belong to.

To accept the Lord means to accept His ways as our ways. We have taken His Word and His teachings as the guide in our lives. To accept Christ means that I accept His rejection as my rejection. When I accept Him I knowingly and willingly accept His cross as my cross. I accept His life as my life—back from the dead I come and up into a different kind of life. It means that I accept His future as my future.

I am talking about the necessity of an exclusive attachment to His person—that is what it means to accept Christ. If the preachers would tell people what it actually means to accept Christ and receive Him and obey Him and live for Him we would have fewer converts but those who would come and commit would not backslide and founder. They would stick.

Actually, preachers and ministers of the gospel of Christ should remember that they are going to stand before the judgment seat of Christ, and they will have to tell a holy Savior why they betrayed His people in this way.

Now, please do not go out and tell people that Mr. Tozer says you should never use those words, "accept Christ." I have tried to make it plain that we should always invite those who are not Christians to come to Jesus, to believe what God says about the Savior, to receive Him by faith into their lives and to obey Him; and to accept Christ as their Savior if they know what it means—an exclusive attachment to the person of Christ.

TO ALL WHO RECEIVED HIM

*He came to that which was his own, but his own did not
receive him. Yet to all who did receive him, to those who
believed in his name, he gave the right to become children
of God—children born not of natural descent, nor of
human decision or a husband's will, but born of God.*

JOHN 1:11–13

S uch a text cannot be properly handled without getting into
areas that some may consider radical. It cannot be handled
without considering the fact that there are many people in the
world who are God's *creation* but not God's *children*. It cannot
be handled without an admission that we do truly believe in the
Fatherhood of God and the brotherhood of man. (Stay with me
and see what the Word of God says about these concepts!) It
cannot be handled without considering the refusal of many "believing Christians" to accept the terms of true discipleship—the

willingness to turn our backs on everything worldly for Jesus' sake. It cannot be handled without discussing the fact that receiving Jesus Christ as Savior and Lord must be an aggressive act of the total personality and not a passive "acceptance" that makes a door-to-door salesman of the Savior. And it certainly cannot be handled without a warning that evangelical Christianity is on a dead-end street if it is going to continue to accept religious activity as a legitimate proof of spirituality.

In this text, God informs us about certain people being born. That is significant. God has stepped out of His way to talk about certain persons being born, and we know that He never does anything without purpose. Everything He does is alive, meaningful, and brilliantly significant. Why should the great God Almighty, who rounded the earth in the hollow of His hand, who set the sun shining in the heavens and flung the stars to the farthest corner of the night—why should this God take important lines in the Bible record to talk about people being born?

There is much for us to consider here, for we generally think of human birth as a very ordinary thing. There are so many babies born in this world every day that it is nothing great—except to the parents and a few close relatives or friends! But the only way to get into this world is to be born. Tales about sliding down a sunbeam or coming in on the wings of a stork do not work. All of us have been born at least once.

Our Lord Jesus Christ was one of the most realistic teachers who ever lived, and here the Scriptures speak about people being "born . . . of the flesh," and as a result of "human decision" and "a husband's will"—the socially accepted rite of marriage and the biological urge that is behind every birth. That is the level of life on which we are born.

No, there is nothing especially remarkable in someone's being born, and yet here is God, prompting an apostle to talk about it. He has it recorded by divine inspiration in His Book, preserved at great cost of blood and tears and toil and prayers for nearly two thousand years. He gives it to us through translators in familiar English. It is a message that certain people are born, and the reason that it is significant and not ordinary is that these appear of a mystic birth, having nothing whatever to do with the physical birth about which we know.

John says plainly that it is a birth on another level; it is not on the blood level. He says that it is a birth that does not have anything to do with blood or bones or tissue. It is a birth that does not have behind it the urge of the flesh or the social arrangement that we call marriage.

AN ACT OF GOD

This invisible birth of which John speaks is an act of God. John is talking about something beyond the physical birth that we know. The senses can touch the physical birth. When we were born into this world, those around us could see and feel and hold and weigh us. They could wash and clothe and feed us. But this invisible, mysterious birth of which John speaks has nothing to do with the flesh. It is of heaven. This birth is of the Spirit—a birth of another kind, a mystic birth.

Some people are very perturbed when a preacher uses the word mystic. They want to chase him out immediately and replace him with a man who is just as much afraid of the word as they are. I am not afraid of the word mystic because the whole Bible is a mystical book, a book of mystery, a book of wonder. I have discovered that you cannot trace any simple phenomenon back very far without coming up against mystery and darkness. It is much more so on the spiritual level.

These of whom the apostle speaks had a mystical birth—a birth of the Spirit altogether contrary to any kind of birth that anyone knew in the physical sense. If Jesus our Lord had talked merely about people being born physically into the world, He would never have been heard, and His teachings would not have been preserved in print. Physical birth is too common— everyone is born. But these people experienced a birth not of the body but of the heart. They were born not into time but into eternity. They were born not of earth but of heaven.

They had an inward birth, a spiritual birth, a mysterious birth, a mystical birth!

A PARTICULAR GRANT OF GOD

This invisible birth is also a particular grant of God. I know there is a sense in which the sovereign God is over all. I like to think that there is not a child born anywhere in the world whom God does not own as His creation. One of our philosophers has said that there are no illegitimate children—only illegitimate parents. In this sense, even those who are born without benefit of clergy or the formalities of a wedding are nevertheless owned by God Almighty as His creation. But that is down on the level of nature, and it is not what our Lord was talking about when He told Nicodemus, "Ye must be born again" (John 3:7).

This other birth—this mysterious, spiritual birth—was by a particular grant. It was altogether other than, different from and superior to the first kind of birth. This new birth is one that gives an unusual right: the right to be born into God's household and thus become a child of the Father.

Now, when I spoke earlier about believing in the Fatherhood of God, I was referring to the fact that God is the Father of all who believe. He is the Father from whom the whole family in heaven and on earth derives its name. But God is not the Father of the sinner. I do not foolishly stretch His Fatherhood to cover all mankind, for God is not the Father of murderers and the immoral. God is the Father of those who believe. I shall not let the liberal and the modernist back me up against a wall and make me deny the Fatherhood of God. Furthermore, I believe in the brotherhood of man. God has made of one blood all people who dwell on the face of the earth. All who are born into the world are born of the same blood. Our skin may be different. Some will have blond hair and some black, some curly and some straight. We may differ from each other greatly in appearance, but there is nevertheless a vast human brotherhood—all of us descended from that man Adam whose mortal sin brought death and all its fruits into the world.

But there is another brotherhood within that brotherhood. It is the brotherhood of the saints of God, for the fact that there is a broad human brotherhood does not mean that all men are saved. They are not. Not until they are saved—born again—do they enter into the brotherhood of the redeemed.

This is where the liberal and the modernist make their mistake. They insist that because mankind is a brotherhood, we are all the children of one Father, and therefore we are all saved. That is nonsense; it is unscriptural and it is not true!

I disagree with the liberal who wants to reduce everyone to a single level—Christian and non-Christian, religious and irreligious, saved and lost, believer and doubter. I believe there is a brotherhood of man that comes by the first birth and another brotherhood that comes through the second birth. By the grace of God, I want to dwell in that sacred, mystic brotherhood of the ransomed and the redeemed, that fellowship of the saints gathered around the broken body and the shed blood of the Savior!

So it is a mysterious birth, and it gives us a particular privilege. "But as many as received him, to them gave he power to become the sons of God" (John 1:12). It is a gift. God gives us the privilege—the legal right—to become children of God. This is what is meant by a person's being born into the kingdom of God. The Bible actually says that God has *given us the privilege of being born*, and this is not just poetry. Sometimes we use a poetic phrase and a person has to edit it down and squeeze the water out of it as well as the air and get it down to a germ of truth to find out what it means. But this is not poetry—this is theology! "He gave [them] the right to become children of God."

THIS BIRTH IS NEWSWORTHY

In the light of so amazing a statement, we can understand why these people of the new birth merited the news item, why they got the byline, why God Almighty put it in His Book that certain people were born in a special way and not just after the flesh. These were the privileged; they had a right given to them that did not belong to others—the right to be the children of God. So it is plain that a person who is a creation of God becomes a child of God only when he or she is born by a special privilege or grant of God Almighty.

It should be of interest to us that this is a right and a privilege that even the angels do not have. Actually, there is a time coming when Christian believers will no longer feel like saluting before any broad-winged angel in heaven. The Scriptures tell us that God has made Jesus for a little time lower than the angels in order that He might taste death for every man. But originally, Jesus was not lower than angels. In fact, God said of Jesus, "And let all the angels of God worship him" (Heb. 1:6).

The promise to us is this: what Jesus is, we will be. Not in a sense of deity, certainly, but in all the rights and privileges. In standing we will be equal to Jesus and like Him, for we shall see Him as He is. In that day, if there is any saluting and bowing to be done, the angels will do it, for the children of the Most High God have the high grant of being like Jesus.

Why do we not actually believe that? We do not half believe it! If we did, we would begin to act like it, in preparation for the great day. I cannot understand why we do not begin to act like children of God if we believe that we have a special higher right to be children of God. We have a right to be sick inside when we see children of heaven acting like the sons of earth, acting like children of the world and the flesh, living like Adam and yet saying they believe in a new birth by God's Spirit.

HOW TO HAVE THE PRIVILEGE

Now, how did these people get that privilege? They *believed*, and they *received*. I am going to pass over the *believe* part of it because we have "believed" ourselves into a blind alley in many cases. Many who go around "believing" never really get very much. But these born-again ones, these born of the mystic birth, believed, in that they were not cynics or doubters or pessimists. They took an optimistic, humble, trusting attitude toward Jesus Christ as their Lord and Savior. They received Him, and "as many as received him . . . gave he power" (John 1:12).

Note that this word *receive* is not passive. Passive is when I receive the action; active is when I perform the act. We have come to the religion of passivity in our day. Toward God, everyone is passive. So we "receive" Christ; we make it a passive thing!

But the Bible knows absolutely nothing about passive reception, for the word *receive* is not passive but active. We make the word *receive* into "accept." Everyone goes around asking, "Will you accept Jesus? Will you accept Him?" This makes a brush salesman out of Jesus Christ, as though He meekly stands waiting to know whether we will patronize Him or not. Although we desperately need what He proffers, we are sovereignly deciding whether we will receive Him or not.

Let me repeat, passive reception is unknown in the Bible. There is no hint of it within the confines of sacred Writ. I for one am tired of being told what to believe by people who parrot everybody else. You could put some of the ministers on perches and they would say, "Polly wants a cracker! Good morning!" all in the same tone of voice. If anyone challenges their line in their books and magazines and songs, they look over their religious noses and declare the person is either radical or touched with modernism.

We have been taught that passive acceptance is the equivalent of faith when it is not. In the Greek, this word receive is active, not passive. You can go to any of the modern translations and you will find that they get across the idea of "take" and "took." "As many as took him," says one fine translation, "to them gave he the power to become the sons of God."

AN AGGRESSIVE ACT OF THE TOTAL PERSONALITY

It is *taking* instead of *accepting*. Whether you are layperson or minister, missionary or student, note this well. Receiving Christ savingly is an act of the total personality. It is an act of the mind and of the will and of the affections. It is thus not only an act of the total personality, it is an *aggressive* act of the total personality.

When you bring that thought over into this text, the Holy Spirit is saying of the children of God: "As many as aggressively took Him with their total personality." There is no inference that they could sit and quietly accept. Every part of their being became a hand reaching forth for Jesus Christ. They took Jesus as Savior and Lord with all of their will and affections and feelings and intellect. That is why it says in the Greek: "As many as actively took Him."

Evangelical Christianity is gasping for breath. We happen to have entered a period when it is a popular thing to sing about tears and prayers and believing. You can get a religious phrase kicked around almost anywhere—even right in the middle of a worldly program dedicated to the flesh and the devil. Old Mammon, with two silver dollars for eyes, sits at the top of it, lying about the quality of the products, shamelessly praising actors who ought to be put to work laying bricks. In the middle of it, someone trained in a studio to sound religious will say with an unctuous voice, "Now, our hymn for the week!" So they break in, and the band goes twinkle, twankle, twinkle, twankle, and they sing something that the devil must blush to hear. They call that religion, and I will concede that religion it is. It is not Christianity, and it is not the Holy Spirit. It is not New Testament and it is not redemption. It is simply making capital out of religion.

I still believe, however, that if someone should come along who could make himself heard to thousands instead of to a few hundred, someone with as much oil as intellect and as much power as penetration, we could yet save evangelical Christianity from the dead-end street where it finds itself. I warn you: do not for one second let the crowds, the bustle of religious activity, the surge of religious thinking fool you into supposing that there is a vast amount of spirituality. It is not so.

That is why the meaning of the word received is so important here. "As many as received him"—actively and aggressively took Him. This means a determined exercise of the will. It means to not deny any condition that the Lord lays down. That is something quite different from what we are hearing. They did not come to the Lord and try to make terms, but they came to the Lord and actively took Him on His terms.

MEETING HIS CONDITIONS

This is the child of God, the believer in Christ who will meet any condition the Lord lays down, even to the forsaking of relatives and friends.

"You are getting radical," you protest. Maybe so, but did you ever read the words of Jesus, "If any man come to me, and hate not his father, and mother, and wife, and children, and brethren, and sisters, yea, and his own life also, he cannot be my disciple" (Luke 14:26)? Jesus is asking us to place our love for Him, our Savior, before that of wife, husband, children. And if we do not, He will not have us. That is the sum of the teaching of Jesus on this subject.

"It is cruel—terribly cruel," you object. The living God demands our love and our loyalty, and we call that demand cruel? Actually, hell is so hot that God is still doing all that He can to arouse us and stir us into action. Lot could have been justified had he forsaken that ungodly family of his and gone out alone from Sodom.

Let us get it straight. Jesus Christ does not just offer us salvation as though it is a decoration or a bouquet or some addition to our garb. He says plainly, "Throw off your old rags, strip to the skin! Let Me dress you in the fine clean robes of My righteousness—all Mine. Then, if it means loss of money, lose it! If it means loss of job, lose it! If it means persecution, take it! If it brings the stiff winds of opposition, bow your head into the wind and take it—for My sake!"

To receive Jesus Christ as Lord is not a passive, soft thing—not a predigested kind of religion. It is strong meat! It is such strong meat that God is calling us in this hour to yield everything to Him.

5

OBEDIENCE IS NOT AN OPTION

*As obedient children, do not conform to the
evil desires you had when you lived in ignorance.*

1 PETER 1:14

The Scriptures do not teach that the person of Jesus Christ
nor any of the important offices that God has given Him
can be divided or ignored according to the whims of men.
Therefore, I must be frank in my feeling that a notable heresy
has come into being throughout our evangelical Christian circles—the widely accepted concept that we humans can choose
to accept Christ only because we need Him as Savior and we
have the right to postpone our obedience to Him as Lord as long
as we want to!

This concept has sprung naturally from a misunderstanding
of what the Bible actually says about Christian discipleship and
obedience. It is now found in nearly all of our full gospel literature. I confess that I was among those who preached it before

I began to pray earnestly, to study diligently and meditate with anguish over the whole matter.

I think the following is a fair statement of what I was taught in my early Christian experience and it certainly needs a lot of modifying and a great many qualifiers to save us from being in error. "We are saved by accepting Christ as our Savior; we are sanctified by accepting Christ as our Lord; we may do the first without doing the second!"

The truth is that salvation apart from obedience is unknown in the sacred Scriptures. Peter makes it plain that we are "elect according to the foreknowledge of God the Father, through sanctification of the Spirit, unto obedience" (1 Peter 1:2). What a tragedy that in our day we often hear the gospel appeal made on this kind of basis: "Come to Jesus! You do not have to obey anyone. You do not have to change anything. You do not have to give up anything, alter anything, surrender anything, give back anything—just come to Him and believe in Him as Savior!"

So they come and believe in the Savior. Later on, in a meeting or conference, they will hear another appeal: "Now that you have received Him as Savior, how would you like to take Him as Lord?"

The fact that we hear this everywhere does not make it right. To urge men and women to believe in a divided Christ is bad teaching, for no one can receive half of Christ, or a third of Christ, or a quarter of the person of Christ! We are not saved by believing in an office nor in a work.

I heard well-meaning workers say, "Come and believe on the finished work." That work will not save you. The Bible does not tell us to believe in an office or a work, but to believe on the Lord

Jesus Christ Himself, the person who has done that work and holds those offices.

Now, note again, Peter's emphasis on obedience among the scattered and persecuted Christians of his day. It seems most important to me that Peter speaks of his fellow Christians as "obedient children" (1 Peter 1:14). He was not giving them a command or exhortation to be obedient. In effect, he said, "Assuming that you are believers, I therefore gather that you are also obedient. So now, as obedient children, do so and so."

OBEDIENCE TAUGHT
THROUGHOUT THE BIBLE

Brethren, I would point out that obedience is taught throughout the entire Bible and that true obedience is one of the toughest requirements of the Christian life. Apart from obedience, there can be no salvation, for salvation without obedience is a self-contradictory impossibility. The essence of sin is rebellion against divine authority.

God said to Adam and Eve, "But of the tree of the knowledge of good and evil, thou shalt not eat of it: for in the day that thou eatest thereof thou shalt surely die" (Gen. 2:17). Here was a divine requirement calling for obedience on the part of those who had the power of choice and will. In spite of the strong prohibition, Adam and Eve stretched forth their hands and tasted of the fruit and thus they disobeyed and rebelled, bringing sin upon themselves. Paul writes very plainly and directly in the book of Romans about "one man's disobedience" (Rom. 5:19)— and this is a stern word by the Holy Spirit through the apostle—

by one man's disobedience came the downfall of the human race!

In John's gospel, the Word is very plain and clear that sin is lawlessness, that sin is disobedience to the law of God. Paul's picture of sinners in Ephesians concludes that the people of the world are "the children of disobedience" (Eph. 2:2). Paul certainly means that disobedience characterizes them, conditions them, molds them. Disobedience has become a part of their nature. All of this provides background for the great, continuing question before the human race: "Who is boss?" This breaks down into a series of three questions: "To whom do I belong?" "To whom do I owe allegiance?" and "Who has authority to require obedience of me?"

Now, I suppose of all the people in the world Americans have the most difficult time in giving obedience to anyone or anything. Americans are supposed to be sons of freedom. We ourselves were the outcropping of a revolt. We spawned a revolution, pouring the tea overboard in the Boston harbor. We made speeches and said, "That sound of the clash of arms is carried on every wind that blows from the Boston Commons" and finally, "Give me liberty or give me death!" That is in the American blood, and when anyone says, "You owe obedience," we immediately bristle! In the natural sense, we do not take kindly to the prospect of yielding obedience to anyone. In the same sense, the people of this world have a quick and ready answer to the questions: "To whom do I belong?" and "To whom do I owe obedience?" Their answer is: "I belong to myself. No one has authority to require my obedience!"

WHERE WE DIRECT OUR ALLEGIANCE

Our generation makes a great deal out of this, and we give it the name of "individualism." On the basis of our individuality, we claim the right of self-determination. In an airplane, the pilot who sits at the controls determines where that plane is going. He must determine the destination. Now, if God had made us humans to be mere machines, we would not have the power of self-determination. But since He made us in His own image and made us to be moral creatures, He has given us that power of self-determination. . . . The poet Tennyson must have thought about this for he wrote in his "In Memoriam": "Our wills are ours, we know not how; our wills are ours to make them Thine." Oh, this mystery of a man's free will is far too great for us! Tennyson said, "We know not how." But then he girds himself and continues, "Yes, our wills are ours to make them Thine." And that is the only right we have here to make our wills the wills of God, to make the will of God our will!

We must remember that God is Who He is, and we are what we are. God is the Sovereign and we are the creatures. He is the Creator and therefore He has a right to command us with the obligation that we should obey. It is a happy obligation, I might say, for "[His] yoke is easy, and [His] burden is light" (Matt. 11:30).

Now, this is where I raise the point again of our human insistence that Christ may sustain a divided relationship toward us. This is now so commonly preached that to oppose it or object to it means that you are sticking your neck out and you had best be prepared for what comes. But how can we insist and teach that our Lord Jesus Christ can be our Savior without being our Lord?

How can we continue to teach that we can be saved without any thought of obedience to our Sovereign Lord?

I am satisfied that when man believes on Jesus Christ, he must believe on the whole Lord Jesus Christ—not making any reservation! I am satisfied that it is wrong to look upon Jesus as a kind of divine nurse to whom we can go when sin has made us sick, and after He has helped us, to say "Goodbye"—and go on our own way.

Suppose I slip into a hospital and tell the staff I need a blood transfusion or perhaps an X-ray of my gall bladder. After they have ministered to me and given their services, do I just slip out of the hospital again with a cheery "Goodbye"—as though I owe them nothing and it was kind of them to help me in my time of need? That may sound like a grotesque concept to you, but it does pretty well draw the picture of those who have been taught that they can use Jesus as a Savior in their time of need without owning Him as Sovereign and Lord and without owing Him obedience and allegiance.

BOTH SAVIOR AND LORD

The Bible never in any way gives us such a concept of salvation. Nowhere are we ever led to believe that we can use Jesus as a Savior and now own Him as our Lord. He is the Lord and as the Lord He saves us, because He has all of the offices of Savior and Christ and High Priest and Wisdom and Righteousness and Sanctification and Redemption! He is all of these things and all of these are embodied in Him as Christ the Lord.

My brethren, we are not allowed to come to Jesus Christ as

shrewd, clever operators saying, "We will take this and this, but we won't take that!" We do not come to Him as one who, buying furniture for his house, declares: "I will take this table but I don't want that chair"—dividing it up! No, sir! It is either all of Christ or none of Christ! I believe we need to preach again a whole Christ to the world—a Christ who does not need our apologies, a Christ who will not be divided, a Christ who will either be Lord of all or who will not be Lord at all!

I think it is important to agree that true salvation restores the right of a Creator-creature relationship because it acknowledges God's right to our fellowship and communion. You see, in our time we have over-emphasized the psychology of the sinner's condition. We spend much time describing the woe of the sinner, the grief of the sinner and the great burden he carries. He does have all of these, but we have over-emphasized them until we forget the principal fact—that the sinner is actually a rebel against properly constituted authority! That is what makes sin, sin. We are rebels. We are sons of disobedience. Sin is the breaking of the law and we are in rebellion and we are fugitives from the just laws of God while we are sinners.

By way of illustration, suppose a man escapes from prison. Certainly he will have grief. He is going to be in pain after bumping logs and stones and fences as he crawls and hides away in the dark. He is going to be hungry and cold and weary. His beard will grow long and he will be tired and cramped and cold—all of these will happen, but they are incidental to the fact that he is a fugitive from justice and a rebel against law.

So it is with sinners. Certainly they are heartbroken and they carry a heavy load. Certainly they labor and are heavy-laden. The

Bible takes full account of these things; but they are incidental to the fact that the reason the sinner is what he is, is because he has rebelled against the laws of God and he is a fugitive from divine judgement.

It is that which constitutes the nature of sin; not the fact that he carries a heavy load of misery and sadness and guilt. These things constitute only the outcropping of the sinful nature, but the root of sin is rebellion against God. Does not the sinner say: "I belong to myself—I owe allegiance to no one unless I choose to give it!" That is the essence of sin.

But thankfully, salvation reverses that and restores the former relationship so that the first thing the returning sinner does is to confess: "Father, I have sinned against heaven, and before thee, and am no more worthy to be called thy son: make me as one of thy hired servants" (Luke 15:18–19). Thus, in repentance, we reverse that relationship and we fully submit to the Word of God and the will of God—as obedient children.

Now that happiness of all the moral creatures lies right here, brethren, in the giving of obedience to God. The Psalmist cried out in Psalm 103:21, "Bless ye the LORD, all ye his hosts; ye ministers of his, that do his pleasure." . . . On the other hand, hell is certainly the world of disobedience. Everything else that may be said about hell may be true, but this one thing is the essence—hell is the world of the rebel! Hell is the Alcatraz for the unconstituted rebels who refuse to surrender to the will of God.

I thank God that heaven is the world of God's obedient children. Whatever else we may say of its pearly gates, its golden streets and its jasper walls, heaven is heaven because children of the Most High God find they are in their normal sphere as obedient moral beings. Jesus said there are fire and worms in hell, but that is not the reason it is hell. You might endure worms and fire, but for a moral creature to know and realize that he is where he is because he is a rebel—that is the essence of hell and judgment. It is the eternal world of all the disobedient rebels who have said, "I owe God nothing!"

This is the time given us to decide. Each person makes his own decision as to the eternal world he is going to inhabit.

A SERIOUS DECISION

This is a serious matter of decision. You do not come to this decision as though it were a matter of being interviewed for a job or getting your diploma at a school. We have no basis to believe that we can come casually and sprightly to the Lord Jesus and say, "I have come for some help, Lord Jesus. I understand that You are the Savior so I am going to believe and be saved and then I am going to turn away and think about the other matters of lordship and allegiance and obedience at some time in the future."

I warn you—you will not get help from Him in that way for the Lord will not save those whom He cannot command. He will not divide His offices. You cannot believe on a half-Christ. We take Him for what He is—the anointed Savior and Lord who is King of kings and Lord of lords! He would not be who He is if He saved us and called us and chose us without the understanding that He can also guide and control our lives.

Brethren, I believe in the deeper Christian life and experience—oh, yes! But I believe we are mistaken when we try to add the deeper life to an imperfect salvation, obtained imperfectly by an imperfect concept of the whole thing. Under the working of the Spirit of God through such men as Finney and Wesley, no one would ever dare to rise in a meeting and say, "I am a Christian" if he had not surrendered his whole being to God and had taken Jesus Christ as his Lord. It was only then that he could say, "I am saved!"

Today, we let them say they are saved no matter how imperfect and incomplete the transaction, with the proviso that the deeper Christian life can be tacked on at some time in the future.

Can it be that we really think that we do not owe Jesus Christ our obedience? We have owed Him obedience ever since the second we cried out to Him for salvation, and if we do not give Him that obedience, I have reason to wonder if we are really converted! I see things and I hear of things that Christian people are doing. As I watch them operate within the profession of Christianity I do raise the question of whether they have been truly converted.

Brethren, I believe it is the result of faulty teaching to begin with. They thought of the Lord as a hospital and Jesus as chief of staff to fix up poor sinners that had gotten into trouble!

"Fix me up, Lord," they have insisted, "so that I can go on my own way!"

That is bad teaching, brethren. It is filled with self-deception. Let us look unto Jesus our Lord, high, holy, wearing the crowns, Lord of lords and King of all, having a perfect right to command full obedience from all of His saved people!

6

YOU CANNOT FACE TWO DIRECTIONS

Do two walk together unless they have agreed to do so?

Amos 3:3

C ontrary to what professing Christians like to think, many of God's people are not willing to walk in perfect agreement with Him, and this may explain why so many believers do not have the power of the Spirit, the peace of the Spirit, and many of the other qualities, gifts, and benefits that the Spirit of God brings.

The question is: Are we willing to walk with Him in love and obedience?

The answer is that we cannot walk with Him unless we are agreed; and if we are not agreed, we will not walk with Him in harmony and fruitfulness and blessing.

Many people in the churches who profess that they have an interest in the subject, "How to cultivate the Spirit's companionship," are not really willing to give up all to obtain all. They are not willing to turn completely toward God and walk with Him.

You may remember that John Bunyan, in his great allegorical writings, often mentioned Mr. Facing Bothways, and we ought to know as well as he did that there are a great many Christians who try to accomplish the difficult task of facing in both directions at the same time. They do want Christ, but they also want some of the world. They allow the Lord to disturb their way, but they also disturb the Lord's way, and there is no use talking about being filled with the Spirit and walking in the Spirit unless we are willing to give up all to obtain all!

Now, this old question in the text, "Can two walk together except they be agreed?" is a rhetorical question, equivalent to a positive declaration that two cannot walk together except they be agreed, and the affirmation that if the two walk together, they must in some sense be one.

These two, in order to walk together, must agree that they want to walk together, and they must agree that it is to their advantage to have this companionship together. I think you will see that it all adds up to this: For two to walk together voluntarily, they must in some sense be one. They must be unified on the important issues of their walk and companionship and direction if they are going to be committed to traveling together.

I have discovered that some people are just not ready for this teaching of commitment and consecration and devotion to the highest will of God for their lives. They are still facing both ways. Let me name some of the types of professing Christians who are not ready to give up all to obtain all.

COUNTERFEIT CHRISTIANITY

There are those who are most interested in Christianity for its "insurance" value. Believe it or not, they want the care and protection that God gives them now, and they want avoidance of hell in time of death. They want the guarantee of heaven at last. To get these things, they seem willing to support the church, give to missions, and show a financial interest in other church projects. Amazing, but true! Some people keep on supporting the church, and they even abstain from some gross pleasures because they want protection—they are interested in the insurance value of Christianity. They want what it has to offer. They are not interested in modernism and liberal Christianity—there isn't any insurance value there.

Are you happy that Jesus Christ died for you on the cross because it means that you will not be brought into judgment, having passed from death into life? Are you willing to live reasonably well, giving up some gross pleasures as a premium you are paying for the guarantee that God will bless you while you live and take you home to heaven when you die?

Some Christians do not like to have this proposition stated in this manner—for it sort of lets the truth leak out that sets up another question: If this is the basis for our Christian life, are we any better than some of the non-professing sinners?

Not every sinner is dirty, you know. Not every sinner is a rascal. There are honorable men and good men and honest men—men that will tell the truth even if it hurts. They have no hope of eternal life or of heaven to come. They are not followers of our Lord. I have known fine, ethical, honest men who were not Christians. Actually, I know a man who is so fine and good that everyone wants to make a Christian out of him. He steadfastly refuses and is positive in his statement, "I am not a Christian." He doesn't claim he is winning his way to heaven— he knows he is lost, but he is so good in his life and his ways and his habits that he puts a lot of Christians to shame.

Then, there are those who are not willing because their concept of religion is social and not spiritual. This includes the people who have watered down the religion of the New Testament until it has no strength, no life, no vitality in it. They water it down with their easygoing opinions. They are very broad-minded—in fact, they are so broad-minded that they cannot walk on the narrow way. They are socially-minded. This is as far as religion goes with them. I am not prepared to say dogmatically that they are not saved, but I am prepared to say that they are not ready for what I am talking about. There is no argument with the fact that the gospel of Christ is essentially spiritual, and Christian truth working upon human souls by the Holy Ghost makes Christian men and women spiritual.

In a similar sense, there are those who are more influenced by the world than by the New Testament, and they are not ready for the Holy Spirit. Of these people, we have to say that they are influenced far more by Hollywood than they are by Jerusalem. Their spirit and mode of life is more like Hollywood than it is like Jerusalem. If you were to suddenly set them down in the New Jerusalem, they would not feel at home because their mode, the texture of their mind, has been created for them by [modern] entertainment and not by the things of God!

I am positive that much that passes for the gospel in our day is very little more than a mild case of orthodox religion grafted onto a heart that is sold out to the world in its pleasures and tastes and ambitions.

REAL DISCIPLESHIP

We have magnified grace in this grace-conscious age. We have magnified grace out of all proportion to the place God gives to it in the Bible. We do have now, as Jude predicted "ungodly men, turning the grace of our God into lasciviousness, and denying the only Lord God, and our Lord Jesus Christ" (1:4). We are so afraid that we will reflect upon the all-sufficiency of grace that we do not dare tell Christians that they must live right. Paul wrote his epistles in the Holy Ghost, and he laid down holy, inward ethics, moral rules for the inward Christian. You can read them in Romans, Corinthians, Ephesians, Colossians and Galatians. Read the Sermon on the Mount and the other teachings of Jesus, and you will see that He does expect His people to be clean and pure and right.

Now, I have heard that a Christian brother has said, "Tozer doesn't distinguish between discipleship and salvation. You can be a Christian without being a disciple." Just let me ask: Who said that you can be a Christian without being a disciple? I don't think you can be a Christian without being a disciple. The idea that I can come to the Lord and by grace have all of my sins forgiven and have my name written in heaven, and have the carpenter go to work on a mansion in my Father's house, and at the same time raise hell on my way to heaven is impossible and unscriptural. It cannot be found in the Bible.

We are never saved by our good works, but we are not saved apart from good works. Out of our saving faith in Jesus Christ, there springs immediately goodness and righteousness. Spring is not brought by flowers, but you cannot have spring without flowers. It isn't my righteousness that saves, but the salvation I have received brings righteousness.

I think we must face up to this now—that we must walk in righteousness if we are going on to know the Lord. The man who is not ready to live right is not saved, and he will not be saved, and he will be deceived in that great day. The grace of God that bringeth salvation teaches the heart that we should deny ungodliness and worldly lusts and live soberly and righteously and godly in this present world. There you have the three dimensions of life: *soberly*—that is me; *righteously*—that is my fellow man; and *godly*—that is God. We ought not to make the mistake of thinking that we can be spiritual and not be good.

I cannot believe that a man is on the road to heaven when he is habitually performing the kind of deeds that would logically indicate that he ought to be on his way to hell. How can the two walk together except they be agreed? He is the Holy Spirit, and if I walk an unholy way, how can I be in fellowship with Him?

RENEW YOUR MIND

God reveals to us that our thoughts are a part of us. Someone has said that "thoughts are things," and the Spirit is all-seeking and all-hearing and all-loving and pure. Can you imagine a man with malicious and evil thoughts in his heart having companionship with the loving Holy Spirit? Can you imagine a man bloated with egotism knowing the Holy Spirit in anything like intimacy? Can you imagine a man who is a deceiver having blessed fellowship with the Holy Spirit? Never! My friend, if you are habitually given over to thinking and harboring and savoring dirty thoughts, you are habitually without the communion of the Holy Ghost!

Keep your mind pure. Clean out the sanctuary the way old Hezekiah did. They had dirtied up that sanctuary so when he had taken over, Hezekiah got all of the priests together. It took them days and days but they carried out all of the filth and burned it, threw it over the bank and got rid of it, and then went back and sanctified the temple. Then the blessed God came and they had their worship again.

Our thoughts are the decorations inside the sanctuary where we live. If our thoughts are purified by the blood of Christ, we are living in a clean room, no matter if we are wearing overalls covered with grease. Our thoughts largely decide the mood and weather and climate within our beings, and God considers our thoughts as part of us. They should be thoughts of peace, thoughts of pity and mercy and kindness, thoughts of charity, thoughts of God and the Son of God—these are pure things, good things and high things.

Therefore, if we would cultivate the Spirit's acquaintance, we must have the control of our thoughts. Our mind ought not to be a wilderness in which every kind of unclean thought makes its own way.

Again, for the kind of fellowship we are talking about, seek to know Him in His Word. Remember that the Spirit of God inspired the Word and He will be revealed in the Word. I really have no place in my sympathies for those Christians who neglect the Word or ignore the Word or get revelations apart from the Word. This is the Book of God, after all, and if we know the Book well enough, we will have an answer to every problem in the world.

Every problem that touches us is answered in the Book—stay by the Word! I want to preach the Word, love the Word and make the Word the most important element in my Christian life. Read it much, read it often, brood over it, think over it, meditate over it—meditate on the Word of God day and night. When you are awake at night, think of a helpful verse. When you get up in the morning, no matter how you feel, think of a verse and make the Word of God the important element in your day. The Holy Ghost wrote the Word, and if you make much of the Word, He will make much of you. It is through the Word that He reveals Himself. Between those covers is a living Book. God wrote it and it is still vital and effective and alive. God is in this Book, the Holy Ghost is in this Book, and if you want to find Him, go into this Book.

Let the old saints be our example. They came to the Word of God and meditated. They laid the Bible on the old-fashioned, handmade chair, got down on the old, scrubbed, board floor and meditated on the Word. As they waited, faith mounted. The Spirit and faith illuminated. They had only a Bible with fine print, narrow margins and poor paper, but they knew their Bible better than some of us do with all of our helps.

Let's practice the art of Bible meditation. But please don't grab that phrase and go out and form a club—we are organized to death already. Just meditate. Let us just be plain, thoughtful

Christians. Let us open our Bibles, spread them out on a chair, and meditate on the Word of God. It will open itself to us, and the Spirit of God will come and brood over it.

I do challenge you to meditate, quietly, reverently, prayerfully, for a month. Put away questions and answers and the filling in of blank lines in the portions you haven't been able to understand. Put all of the cheap trash away and take the Bible, get on your knees, and in faith, say, "Father, here I am. Begin to teach me!"

He will surely teach you about Himself and about Jesus and about the Spirit and about life and death and heaven and hell, and about His own presence.

CHOOSE WHICH DIRECTION TO FACE

Now, I recommend that you find out what it is that has been hindering you in your Christian experience. You have not made progress. You do not know God as well as you did. It all depends upon how you must answer certain questions about your daily life and habits—some things you do and others that you are not doing. Do these things help to hide the face of Jesus from you? Do these things chill and stifle your spiritual progress? Do these things take the joy out of your spirit? Do they make the Word of God a little less sweet? Do they make earth more desirable and heaven farther away?

Repentance may be necessary. There may be some necessary cleaning up before the Holy Spirit will come and warm your heart and refresh it and make it fragrant with His presence. This is how we cultivate the Spirit's friendship and companionship.

7

CRUCIFIED
WITH CHRIST

*I have been crucified with Christ and I no longer
live, but Christ lives in me. The life I now live
in the body, I live by faith in the Son of God,
who loved me and gave himself for me.*

GALATIANS 2:20

There seems to be a great throng of professing Christians in our churches today whose total and amazing testimony sounds about like this: "I am thankful for God's plan in sending Christ to the cross to save me from hell." I am convinced that it is a cheap, low-grade, and misleading kind of Christianity that impels people to rise and state, "Because of sin, I was deeply in debt—and God sent His Son, who came and paid all my debts."

Of course, believing Christian men and women are saved from the judgment of hell, and it is a reality that Christ our Redeemer has paid the whole slate of debt and sin that was against us. But what does God say about His purposes in allowing Jesus to go to the cross and to the grave? What does God say about the meaning of death and resurrection for the Christian believer?

Surely, we know the Bible well enough to be able to answer that: God's highest purpose in the redemption of sinful humanity was based in His hope that we would allow Him to reproduce the likeness of Jesus Christ in our once-sinful lives! This is the reason why we should be concerned with this text—this testimony of the apostle Paul in which he shares his own personal theology with the Galatian Christians who had become known for their backslidings. It is a beautiful miniature, shining forth as an unusual and sparkling gem, an entire commentary on the deeper Christian life and experience. We are not trying to take it out of its context by dealing with it alone; we are simply acknowledging the fact that the context is too broad to be dealt with in any one message.

I AM CRUCIFIED

It is the King James Version of the Bible that quotes Paul: "I am crucified with Christ." Nearly every other version quotes Paul as speaking in a different tense: "I have been crucified with Christ," and that really is the meaning of it: "I have been crucified with Christ."

This verse is quoted sometimes by people who have simply memorized it and they would not be able to tell you what Paul was really trying to communicate. This is not a portion of Scripture that can be skipped through lightly. You cannot skim through and pass over this verse as many seem to be able to do with the Lord's Prayer and the twenty-third Psalm.

This is a verse with such depth of meaning and spiritual potential for the Christian believer that we are obligated to seek its full meaning—so it can become practical and workable and liveable in all of our lives in this present world.

It is plain in this text that Paul was forthright and frank in the matter of his own personal involvement in seeking and finding God's highest desires and provision for Christian experience and victory. He was not bashful about the implications of his own personality becoming involved with the claims of Jesus Christ. Not only does he plainly testify, "I have been crucified," but within the immediate vicinity of these verses, he uses the words *I, myself,* and *me* a total of fourteen times.

There certainly is, in the Bible, a good case for humility in the human personality, but it can be overdone. We have had a dear missionary veteran among us from time to time. He is learned and cultured—and overly modest. With a great wealth of missionary exploits and material to tell, he has always refused to use any first person reference to himself. When asked to tell about something that happened in his pioneer missionary life, he said: "One remembers when one was in China and one saw. . . ."

That seems to be carrying the idea of modesty a bit too far, so I said to him, in a joking way, that if he had been writing the twenty-third Psalm, it would likely read: "The Lord is one's shepherd, one shall not want; He maketh one to lie down in green pastures. He leadeth one. . . ."

I believe Paul knew that there is a legitimate time and place for the use of the word I. In spiritual matters, some people seem to want to maintain a kind of anonymity, if possible. As far as they are concerned, someone else should take the first step. This often comes up in the manner of our praying, as well. Some Christians are so general and vague and uninvolved in their requests that God Himself is unable to answer. I refer to the man who will bow his head and pray: "Lord, bless the missionaries and all for whom we should pray. Amen."

It is as though Paul says to us here, "I am not ashamed to use myself as an example. I have been crucified with Christ. I am willing to be pinpointed."

Only Christianity recognizes why the person who is without God and without any spiritual perception gets in such deep trouble with his own ego. When he says I, he is talking about the sum of his own individual being, and if he does not really know who he is or what he is doing here, he is beseiged in his personality with all kinds of questions and problems and uncertainties.

Most of the shallow psychology religions of the day try to deal with the problem of the ego by jockeying it around from one position to another, but Christianity deals with the problem of I by disposing of it with finality.

The Bible teaches that every unregenerated human being will continue to wrestle with the problems of his own natural ego and selfishness. His human nature dates back to Adam. But the Bible also teaches with joy and blessing that every individual may be born again, thus becoming a "new man" in Christ.

When Paul speaks in this text, "I have been crucified," he is saying that "my natural self has been crucified." That is why he can go on to say, "Yet I live"—for he has become another and a new person—"I live in Christ and Christ lives in me."

It is this first I, the natural me, that stands confronted with the just anger of God. God cannot acknowledge and accept me as a natural and selfish man—I am unregenerate and an alien, the complete essence of everything that is anti-God!

NO MIDDLE GROUND

I know there are men and women who dismiss the idea of anything being anti-God or anti-Christ. They are not willing to pay any heed to the teachings of Scripture relative to prophecy and eschatology.

Nevertheless, it is a biblical fact that whatever does not go through the process of crucifixion and transmutation, passing over into the new creation, is anti-Christ. Jesus said that all of that which is not with Christ is against Christ—those who are not on His side are against Him. We do not quite know what to do with those words of Christ, so we try to evade or work them over to a smooth, new version, but Jesus said "he that gathereth not with me scattereth abroad" (Matt. 12:30).

There is a great hue and cry throughout the world today on behalf of tolerance and much of it comes from a rising spirit of godlessness in the nations. The communist nations, themselves the most intolerant, are preaching and calling for tolerance in order to break down all of the borders of religion and embarrass the American people with our social and racial problems.

This is the situation of the people of God: the most intolerant book in all the wide world is the Bible, the inspired Word of God, and the most intolerant teacher that ever addressed Himself to an audience was the Lord Jesus Christ Himself.

On the other hand, Jesus Christ demonstrated the vast difference between being charitable and being tolerant. Jesus Christ was so charitable that in His great heart He took in all the people in the world and was willing to die even for those who hated Him.

But even with that kind of love and charity crowning His being, Jesus was so intolerant that He taught: "If you are not on My side, you are against Me. If you do not believe that I am He, you shall die in your sins." He did not leave any middle ground to accommodate the neutral who preach tolerance. There is no "twilight zone" in the teachings of Jesus—no place in between.

Charity is one thing, but tolerance is quite another matter. Tolerance easily becomes a matter of cowardice if spiritual principles are involved, if the teachings of God's Word are ignored and forgotten.

Suppose we take the position of compromise that many want us to take: "Everyone come, and be saved if you want to. But if you do not want to be saved, maybe there is some other way that we can find for you. We want you to believe in the Lord Jesus Christ if you will, but if you do not want to, there may be a possibility that God will find some other way for you because there are those who say that there are many ways to God."

That would not be a spirit of tolerance on our part—it would be downright cowardice. We would be guilty with so many others of a spirit of compromise that so easily becomes an anti-God attitude.

THE CALLING FOR EVERY CHRISTIAN

True Christianity deals with the human problem of the self-life, with the basic matter of "me, myself, and I." The Spirit of God deals with it by an intolerant and final destruction, saying, "This selfish I cannot live if God is to be glorified in this human life." God Himself deals with this aspect of human nature—the sum of all our proud life—and pronounces a stern condemnation upon it, flatly and frankly disapproving of it, fully and completely rejecting it.

And what does God say about it? "I am God alone, and I will have nothing to do with man's selfish ego, in which I find the essence of rebellion and disobedience and unbelief. Man's nature in its pride of self and egotism is anti-God—and sinful, indeed!" It is in this matter of how to deal with man's proud and perverse and sinful human nature that we discover two positions within the framework of Christianity.

One position is that which leans heavily upon the practice of psychology and psychiatry. There are so-called Christian leaders who insist that Jesus came into the world to bring about an adjustment of our ego, our selfishness, our pride, our perversity. They declare that we may become completely adjusted to life and to one another by dealing with the complexes and the twisted concepts that we have gotten into because our mothers scolded us when we were babies! So, there are thousands of referrals as the clergymen shift our problems from the church to the psychiatric couch.

On the other hand, thank God, the Bible plainly says that Jesus Christ came to bring an end of *self*—not to educate it or tolerate it or polish it! No one can ever say that Jesus Christ came to tell us how to cultivate our natural ego and pride. Jesus never taught that we could learn to get along with the big, proud I in our lives by giving it a love for Bach and Beethoven and Da Vinci.

Paul outlined the full spiritual remedy: "I am crucified with

Christ . . . and the life which I now live in the flesh I live by the faith of the Son of God, who loved me, and gave Himself for me." This is a decision and an attitude of faith and commitment called for in the life of every believing Christian.

When we see that Jesus Christ came into the world to deal effectively and finally with our life of self and egotism and pride, we must take a stand. With God's help, we say to that big I in our nature: "This is as far as you go—you are deposed. You are no longer to be in control!" In true repentance and in self-repudiation, we may turn our backs on the old self life. We may refuse to go along with it any longer. We have the right and the power to desert its ranks and cross over to spiritual victory and blessing on Emmanuel's side, walking joyfully under the banner of the cross of Jesus Christ from that hour on.

This is what it means to deal with and finally dispose of the "old man," the old life of self, which is still causing problems in so many Christian lives. We take a place of actual identification with Jesus Christ in His crucifixion, burial, and resurrection.

In the Christian life, that is what baptism is supposed to mean, but sad to say, baptism is nothing but a quick dip to the average person because that one does not know what baptism represents. He does not know that baptism genuinely ought to be an outward and visible testimony of a spiritual and inward transformation that has taken place; a symbol declaring that the old selfish and perverse human nature is repudiated in humility, and put away, crucified, declared dead!

That is what baptism should mean to the believer—death and burial with Christ, then raised with Him in the power of His resurrection! It can happen apart from water baptism of any mode, but that is what water baptism should indicate. It should set forth that identification with the death and resurrection of Jesus Christ just as a wedding ring witnesses and sets forth the fact that you are married.

IDENTIFICATION WITH JESUS

Now, it is impossible to bring together and synchronize these two positions concerning the old life and nature of self. I do not believe that we are ever obliged to dovetail these two positions. Either the Lord Jesus Christ came to bring an end of self and reveal a new life in spiritual victory, or He came to patch and repair the old self—He certainly did not come to do both!

I expect someone to say, "We are interested in spiritual victory and blessing in our group, but our approach doesn't agree with yours at all!"

In answer I can only say that on the basis of the Word of God, true identification with Jesus Christ in His death, burial and resurrection will lead men and women to Christlikeness. God has never promised to work out His image in us in a variety of ways according to the inclinations of our own group. Forming the likeness to Jesus Christ in human lives and personalities is something that He does alike in all groups and all conferences and all fellowships around the world regardless of what they may be called.

There really is no way to patch up and repair the old life of self. The whole burden of New Testament theology insists that the old human self is ruined completely. It has no basic goodness, it holds to false values and its wisdom is questionable, to say the least. It is the new self in Christ Jesus—the new man in Christ—that alone must live. Onward from the point of this commitment, we must reckon ourselves indeed to have died unto sin, to be alive unto God in Christ Jesus. . . .

Human beings continue to lean on a variety of crutches to support the ego, to nourish the pride, to cover the obvious defects in human existence. Many have believed that continuing education would provide that missing link between personality and potential. Many have turned to the pursuits of philosophies; others to cultural achievements. Ancestry and environment and status occupy many more.

But the ability to brag about human ancestors, to point with pride to the nation of our descent or the cultural privileges we have known—these do not transform and change and regenerate the human nature. Regardless of our racial strains, regardless of our cultural and educational advantages, we are all alike as human beings. In my own nature, I am nothing. Of myself, I know nothing. In God's sight, without His help and His enabling, I have nothing and I can do nothing.

But the inventory of the new man in Christ Jesus is so different! If he has found the meaning of commitment, the giving up of self to be identified with Jesus Christ in His crucifixion and death, he discovers in an entirely new measure the very presence of Christ Himself!

This new person has made room for the presence of Christ, so there is a difference in the personal inventory. It is no longer the old do-nothing, know-nothing, be-nothing, have-nothing person! That old assertive self died when the crucified and risen Savior was given His rightful place of command and control in the personality. The old inventory cried out: "How can I be what I ought to be?" but the inventory of the new man is couched in faith and joy in his recognition that "Christ liveth in me!"

Paul expressed it to the Colossians in this way: "Christ in you, the hope of glory!" and then proceeded to assure them that "You are complete in Him!"

Paul wrote to the Ephesians to remind them that the essence of faith and hope in Christ is the assurance of being "accepted in the Beloved."

To the Corinthian believers, Paul promised full spiritual deliverance and stability in the knowledge that Jesus Christ "is made unto us wisdom, righteousness, sanctification and redemption."

Our great need, then, is simply Jesus Christ. He is what we need. He has what we need. He knows what we need to know. He has the ability to do in us what we cannot do—working in us that which is well-pleasing in God's sight.

BECOMING LIKE CHRIST

This is a difficult point in spiritual doctrine and life for many people.

"What about my ambition? I have always been ambitious so it is a part of my being. Doesn't it matter?"

"I am used to doing my own thing in my own way—and I am still doing it in the church. Do I have to yield that?"

"I have always been able to put my best foot forward to get recognition and publicity. I am used to seeing my name in the paper. What do I get from crucifixion with Christ?"

Brothers and sisters, you get Christ and glory and fruitfulness and future and the world to come, whereof we speak, and the spirits of just men made perfect; you get Jesus, the Mediator of a new covenant, and the blood of the everlasting covenant; an innumerable company of angels and the church of the firstborn and the New Jerusalem, the city of the living God!

And before you get all that, you have the privilege and the prospect of loving and joyful service for Christ and for mankind on this earth.

This is a gracious plan and provision for men and women in the kindness and wisdom of God. He loves you too well and too much to let you continue to strut and boast and cultivate your egotism and feed your I. He just cannot have that kind of selfish assertion in His children, so Jesus Christ works in us to complete Himself and make Himself anew in us.

So, you see, that is really why Jesus Christ came into this world to tabernacle with us, to die for us. God is never going to be done with us in shaping us and fashioning us as dear children of God until the day that we will see Him face to face, and His name shall be in our foreheads. In that day, we shall genuinely be like Him and we shall see Him as He is.

Truly, in that gracious day, our rejoicing will not be in the personal knowledge that He saved us from hell, but in the joyful knowledge that He was able to renew us, bringing the old self to an end, and creating within us the new man and the new self in which can be reproduced the beauty of the Son of God.

In the light of that provision, I think it is true that no Christian is where he ought to be spiritually until that beauty of the Lord Jesus Christ is being reproduced in daily Christian life. I admit that there is necessarily a question of degree in this kind of transformation of life and character.

Certainly there has never been a time in our human existence when we could look into our own being, and say: "Well, thank God, I see it is finished now. The Lord has signed the portrait. I see Jesus in myself!"

Nobody will say that—nobody!

Even though a person has become like Christ, he will not know it. He will be charitable and full of love and peace and grace and mercy and kindness and goodness and faithfulness—but he will not really know it because humility and meekness are also a part of the transformation of true godliness. Even though he is plainly God's man and Christ's witness, he will be pressing on, asking folks to pray for him, reading his Bible with tears, and saying, "Oh, God, I want to be like Thy Son!"

God knows that dear child is coming into the likeness of His Son, and the angels know it, and the observing people around him know it, too. But he is so intent upon the will and desires of God for his life and personality that he does not know it, for true humility never looks in on itself. Emerson wrote that the eye that sees only itself is blind and that the eye is not to see with but to see through. If my eye should suddenly become conscious of itself, I would be a blind man.

Now, there is a practical application of the crucified life and its demands from day to day. John the Baptist realized it long ago when he said, "He must increase but I must decrease!"

There must necessarily be less and less of me—and more and more of Christ! That's where you feel the bite and the bitterness of the cross, brother! Judicially and potentially, I was crucified with Christ, and now God wants to make it actual. In actuality, it is not as simple as that. Your decision and commitment do not then allow you to come down from that cross. Peace and power and fruitfulness can only increase according to our willingness to confess moment by moment, "It is no longer I, but Christ that liveth in me."

God is constantly calling for decisions among those in whom there is such great potential for displaying the life of Jesus Christ. We must decide: "My way, or Christ's?" Will I insist upon my own righteousness even while God is saying that it must be the righteousness of His Son? Can I still live for my own honor and praise? No, it must be for Christ's honor and praise to be well-pleasing to God. "Do I have any choice? Can I have my own plan?" No, God can only be honored as we make our choices in Christ and live for the outworking of God's plan.

MY KINGDOM GO

Modern theology refuses to press down very hard at this point, but we still are confronted often with spiritual choices in our hymnology. We often sing: "Oh, to be dead to myself, dear Lord; Oh, to be lost in Thee."

We sing the words, we soon shut the book, and drift away with friends to relax and have a pleasant soda. The principle does not become operative in most Christians. It does not become practical. That is why I keep saying and teaching and hoping that this principle that is objective truth will become subjective experience in Christian lives. For any professing Christian who dares to say, "Knowing the truth is enough for me; I do not want to mix it up with my day-to-day life and experience," Christianity has become nothing but a farce and a delusion!

It may surprise you that Aldous Huxley, often a critic of orthodox and evangelical Christianity, has been quoted as saying: "My kingdom go is the necessary correlary to *Thy* kingdom *come*."

How many Christians are there who pray every Sunday in church, "Thy kingdom come! Thy will be done!" without ever realizing the spiritual implications of such intercession? What are we praying for? Should we edit that prayer so that it becomes a confrontation: "My kingdom go, Lord; let Thy kingdom come!" Certainly His kingdom can never be realized in my life until my own selfish kingdom is deposed. It is when I resign, when I am no longer king of my domain that Jesus Christ will become king of my life.

Now, brethren, in confession, may I assure you that a Christian clergyman cannot follow any other route to spiritual victory and daily blessing than that which is prescribed so plainly in the Word of God. It is one thing for a minister to choose a powerful text, expound it and preach from it—it is quite something else for the minister to honestly and genuinely live forth the meaning of the Word from day to day. A clergyman is a man—and often he has a proud little kingdom of his own, a kingdom of position and often of pride and sometimes with power. Clergymen must wrestle with the spiritual implications of the crucified life just like everyone else, and to be thoroughgoing men of God and spiritual examples to the flock of God, they must die daily to the allurements of their own little kingdoms of position and prestige.

One of the greatest of the pre-Reformation preachers in Germany was Johannes Tollar, certainly an evangelical before

Luther's time. The story has been told that a devout layman, a farmer whose name was Nicholas, came down from the countryside, and implored Dr. Tollar to preach a sermon in the great church, dealing with the deeper Christian life based on spiritual union with Jesus Christ.

The following Sunday Dr. Tollar preached that sermon. It had 26 points, telling the people how to put away their sins and their selfishness in order to glorify Jesus Christ in their daily lives. It was a good sermon—actually, I have read it and I can underscore every line of it.

When the service was over and the crowd had dispersed, Nicholas came slowly down the aisle.

He said, "Pastor Tollar, that was a great sermon and I want to thank you for the truth which you presented. But I am troubled and I would like to make a comment, with your permission."

"Of course, and I would like to have your comment," the preacher said.

"Pastor, that was great spiritual truth that you brought to the people today, but I discern that you were preaching it to others as truth without having experienced the implications of deep spiritual principles in your own daily life," Nicholas told him. "You are not living in full identification with the death and resurrection of Jesus Christ. I could tell by the way you preached—I could tell!"

The learned and scholarly Dr. Tollar did not reply. But he was soon on his knees, seeking God in repentance and humiliation. For many weeks he did not take the pulpit to preach—earnestly seeking day after day the illumination of the Spirit of God in order that objective truth might become a deep and renewing and warming spiritual experience within.

After the long period of the dark sufferings in his soul, the day came when John Tollar's own kingdom was brought to an end and was replaced by God's kingdom. The great flood of the Spirit came in on his life and he returned to his parish and to his pulpit to become one of the greatest and most fervent and effective preachers of his generation. God's gracious blessings came—but Tollar first had to die. This is what Paul meant when he said, "I have been crucified with Christ."

This must become living reality for all of us who say we are interested in God's will for our lives. You pray for me and I will surely pray for you—because this is a matter in which we must follow our Lord!

We can quote this text from memory, but that is not enough. I can say that I know what Paul meant, but that is not enough. God promises to make it living reality in our lives the instant that we let our little, selfish kingdom go!

TAKE UP
YOUR CROSS

*Whoever wants to be my disciple must deny
themselves and take up their cross and follow me.*

Matthew 16:24

I t is like the Lord to fasten a world upon nothing, and make it stay in place. Here He takes that wonderful, mysterious microcosm we call the human soul and makes its future well-being or suffering to rest upon a single word—*if.* "If any man," He says and teaches at once the universal inclusiveness of His invitation and the freedom of the human will. Everyone may come; no one need come, and whoever does come, comes because he chooses to.

Every man holds his future in his hand. Not the dominant world leader only, but the inarticulate man lost in anonymity is a "man of destiny." He decides which way his soul shall go. He chooses, and destiny waits on the nod of his head. He decides, and hell enlarges herself, or heaven prepares another mansion. So much of Himself has God given to men.

THE WORK OF SEPARATION

There is a strange beauty in the ways of God with men. He sends salvation to the world in the person of a Man and sends that Man to walk the busy ways saying, "If any man will come after me." No drama, no fanfare, no tramp of marching feet or tumult of shouting. A kindly Stranger walks through the earth, and so quiet is His voice that it is sometimes lost in the hurly-burly; but it is the last voice of God, and until we become quiet to hear it we have no authentic message. He bears good tidings from afar but He compels no man to listen. "If any man will," He says, and passes on. Friendly, courteous, unobtrusive, He yet bears the signet of the King. His word is divine authority, His eyes a tribunal, His face a last judgment.

"If any man will come after me," He says, and some will rise and go after Him, but others give no heed to His voice. So the gulf opens between man and man, between those who will and those who will not. Silently, terribly the work goes on, as each one decides whether he will hear or ignore the voice of invitation. Unknown to the world, perhaps unknown even to the individual, the work of separation takes place. Each hearer of the Voice must decide for himself, and he must decide on the basis of the evidence the message affords. There will be no thunder sound, no heavenly sign or light from heaven. The Man is His own proof. The marks in His hands and feet are the insignia of His rank and office. He will not put Himself again on trial; He will not argue, but the morning of the judgment will confirm what men in the twilight have decided.

THE CONDITIONS

And those who would follow Him must accept His conditions. "Let him," He says, and there is no appeal from His words. He will use no coercion, but neither will He compromise. Men cannot make the terms; they merely agree to them. Thousands turn from Him because they will not meet His conditions. He watches them as they go, for He loves them, but He will make no concessions. Admit one soul into the kingdom by compromise and that kingdom is no longer secure. Christ will be Lord, or He will be Judge. Every man must decide whether he will take Him as Lord now or face Him as Judge then.

What are the terms of discipleship? Only one with a perfect knowledge of mankind could have dared to make them. Only the Lord of men could have risked the effect of such rigorous demands: "Let him deny himself." We hear these words and shake our heads in astonishment. Can we have heard aright? Can the Lord lay down such severe rules at the door of the kingdom? He can and He does. If He is to save the man, He must save him from himself. It is the "himself" that has enslaved and corrupted the man. Deliverance comes only by denial of that self. No man in his own strength can shed the chains with which self has bound him, but in the next breath the Lord reveals the source of the power which is to set the soul free: "Let him . . . take up his cross." The cross has gathered in the course of the years much of beauty and symbolism, but the cross of which Jesus spoke had nothing of beauty in it. It was an instrument of death. Slaying men was its only function. Men did not wear that cross; but that cross wore men. It stood naked until a man was pinned on it, a

101

living man fastened like some grotesque stickpin on its breast to writhe and groan till death stilled and silenced him. That is the cross. Nothing less. And when it is robbed of its tears and blood and pain it is the cross no longer. "Let him . . . take up his cross," said Jesus, and in death he will know deliverance from himself.

A strange thing under the sun is crossless Christianity. The cross of Christendom is a no-cross, an ecclesiastical symbol. The cross of Christ is a place of death. Let each one be careful which cross he carries.

"And follow me." Now the glory begins to break in upon the soul that has just returned from Calvary. "Follow me" is an invitation and a challenge and a promise. The cross has been the end of a life and the beginning of a life. The life that ended there was a life of sin and slavery; the life that began there is a life of holiness and spiritual freedom. "And follow me," He says, and faith runs on tiptoe to keep pace with the advancing light. Until we know the program of our risen Lord for all the years to come we can never know everything He meant when He invited us to follow Him. Each heart can have its own dream of fair worlds and new revelations, of the odyssey of the ransomed soul in the ages to come, but whoever follows Jesus will find at last that He has made the reality to outrun the dream.

EACH ONE'S OWN CROSS

Crosses are all alike, but no two are identical. Never before nor since has there been a cross experience just like that endured by the Savior. The whole dreadful work of dying which Christ suffered was something unique in the experience of mankind. It had to be so if the cross was to mean life for the world. The sin bearing, the darkness, the rejection by the Father were agonies peculiar to the person of the holy sacrifice. To claim any experience remotely like that of Christ would be more than an error; it would be sacrilege.

Every cross was and is an instrument of death, but no man could die on the cross of another; each man died on his own cross; hence Jesus said, "Let him . . . take up *his* cross daily, and follow me" (Luke 9:23, emphasis added).

Now there is a real sense in which the cross of Christ embraces all crosses and the death of Christ encompasses all deaths. "For the love of Christ constraineth us; because we thus judge, that if one died for all, then were all dead" (2 Cor. 5:14). "I am crucified with Christ" (Gal. 2:20). "Save in the cross of our Lord Jesus Christ, by whom the world is crucified unto me, and I unto the world" (6:14). This is in the judicial working of God in redemption. The Christian as a member of the Body of Christ is crucified along with his divine Head. Before God every true believer is reckoned to have died when Christ died. All subsequent experience of personal crucifixion is based upon this identification with Christ on the cross.

But in the practical, everyday outworking of the believer's crucifixion his own cross is brought into play. "Let him . . . take up *his* cross daily" (emphasis added). That is obviously not the cross of Christ. Rather, it is the believer's own personal cross by means of which the cross of Christ is made effective in slaying his evil nature and setting him free from its power.

The believer's own cross is one he has assumed voluntarily. Therein lies the difference between his cross and the cross on which Roman convicts died. They went to the cross against their will; he, because he chooses to do so. No Roman officer ever pointed to a cross and said, "If any man will, let him." Only Christ said that, and by so saying He placed the whole matter in the hands of the Christian. He can refuse to take his cross, or he can stoop and take it up and start for the dark hill. The difference between great sainthood and spiritual mediocrity depends upon which choice he makes.

To go along with Christ step by step and point by point in identical suffering of Roman crucifixion is not possible for any of us and certainly is not intended by our Lord. What He does intend is that each of us should count himself dead indeed with Christ and then accept willingly whatever of self-denial, repentance, humility, and humble sacrifice that may be found in the path of obedient daily living. That is his cross, and it is the only one the Lord has invited him to bear.

9

LOVING RIGHTEOUSNESS, HATING EVIL

You have loved righteousness and hated wickedness.

HEBREWS 1:9

The message to first-century Hebrew Christians was precise and direct: Let Jesus Christ be your motivation to love righteousness and to hate iniquity. In our present century, our spiritual obligations and responsibilities are no different. The character and attributes of Jesus, the eternal Son, have not changed and will not change.

> But unto the Son he saith, Thy throne, O God, is for ever and ever: a sceptre of righteousness is the sceptre of thy kingdom. Thou hast loved righteousness, and hated iniquity; therefore God, even thy God, hath anointed thee with the oil of gladness above thy fellows. (Heb. 1:8–9)

. . . When Jesus was on earth, He was not the passive, color-less, spineless person He is sometimes made out to be in paintings and literature. He was a strong man, a man of iron will. He was able to love with an intensity of love that burned Him up. He was able to hate with the strongest degree of hatred against everything that was wrong and evil and selfish and sinful.

Invariably someone will object when I make a statement like that. "I cannot believe such things about Jesus. I always thought it was a sin to hate!" Study long and well the record and the teachings of Jesus while He was on earth. In them lies the answer. It is a sin for the children of God not to hate what ought to be hated. Our Lord Jesus loved righteousness, but He hated iniquity. I think we can say He hated sin and wrong and evil perfectly!

If we are committed, consecrated Christians, truly disciples of the crucified and risen Christ, there are some things we must face. We cannot love honesty without hating dishonesty. We cannot love purity without hating impurity. We cannot love truth without hating lying and deceitfulness.

If we belong to Jesus Christ, we must hate evil even as He hated evil in every form. The ability of Jesus Christ to hate that which was against God and to love that which was full of God was the force that made Him able to receive the anointing—the oil of gladness—in complete measure. On our human side, it is our imperfection in loving the good and hating the evil that prevents us from receiving the Holy Spirit in complete measure. God withholds from us because we are unwilling to follow Jesus in His great poured-out love for what is right and His pure and holy hatred of what is evil.

HATE SIN, LOVE THE SINNER

This question always arises: "Did our Lord Jesus Christ hate sinners?" We already know the answer. He loved the world. We know better than to think that Jesus hated any sinner. Jesus never hated a sinner, but He hated the evil and depravity that controlled the sinner. He did not hate the proud Pharisee, but He detested the pride and self-righteousness of the Pharisee. He did not hate the woman taken in adultery. But he acted against the harlotry that made her what she was.

Jesus hated the devil and He hated those evil spirits that He challenged and drove out. We present-day Christians have been misled and brainwashed, at least in a general way, by a generation of soft, pussycat preachers. They would have us believe that to be good Christians we must be able to purr softly and accept everything that comes along with Christian tolerance and understanding. Such ministers never mention words like *zeal* and *conviction* and *commitment*. They avoid phrases like "standing for the truth."

I am convinced that a committed Christian will show a zealous concern for the cause of Christ. He or she will live daily with a set of spiritual convictions taken from the Bible. He or she will be one of the toughest to move—along with a God-given humility—in his or her stand for Christ. Why, then, have Christian ministers so largely departed from exhortations to love righteousness with a great, overwhelming love, and to hate iniquity with a deep, compelling revulsion?

WHY NO PERSECUTION?

People remark how favored the church is in this country. It does not have to face persecution and rejection. If the truth were known, our freedom from persecution is because we have taken the easy, popular way. If we would love righteousness until it became an overpowering passion, if we would renounce everything that is evil, our day of popularity and pleasantness would quickly end. The world would soon turn on us.

We are too nice! We are too tolerant! We are too anxious to be popular! We are too quick to make excuses for sin in its many forms! If I could stir Christians around me to love God and hate sin, even to the point of being a bit of a nuisance, I would rejoice. If some Christian were to call me for counsel saying he or she is being persecuted for Jesus' sake, I would say with feeling, "Thank God!"

Vance Havner used to remark that too many are running for something when they ought to be standing for something. God's people should be willing to stand! We have become so brainwashed in so many ways that Christians are afraid to speak out against uncleanness in any form. The enemy of our souls has persuaded us that Christianity should be a rather casual thing— certainly not something to get excited about.

Fellow Christian, we have only a little time. We are not going to be here very long. Our triune God demands that we engage in those things that will remain when the world is on fire, for fire determines the value and quality of every person's work.

I have shared these things with you because I am of the opinion that the glad oil, the blessed anointing of the Holy Spirit, is not having opportunity to flow freely among church members of our day. We can hardly expect any such spiritual movement among those who proudly class themselves as liberals. They reject the deity of Christ, the inspiration of the Bible and the divine ministries of the Holy Spirit. How can the oil of God flow among and bless those who do not believe in such an oil of gladness?

But what about us of the evangelical persuasion with our biblical approach to fundamental New Testament truth and teaching? We must ask ourselves why the oil of God is not flowing very noticeably around us. We have the truth. We believe in the anointing and the unction. Why is the oil not flowing?

WE ARE TOLERANT OF EVIL

I think the reason is that we are tolerant of evil. We allow what God hates because we want to be known to the world as good-natured, agreeable Christians. Our stance indicates that the last thing we would want anyone to say about us is that we are narrow-minded. The way to spiritual power and favor with God is to be willing to put away the weak compromises and the tempting evils to which we are prone to cling. There is no Christian victory or blessing if we refuse to turn away from the things that God hates.

Even if your wife loves it, turn away from it.

Even if your husband loves it, turn away from it.

Even if it is accepted in the whole social class and system of which you are a part, turn away from it.

Even if it is something that has come to be accepted by our

whole generation, turn away from it if it is evil and wrong and an offense to our holy and righteous Savior.

I am being as frank and as searching as I can possibly be. I know that we lack the courage and the gladness that should mark the committed people of God. And that concerns me. Deep within the human will with which God has endowed us, every Christian holds the key to his or her own spiritual attainment. If he or she will not pay the price of being joyfully led by the Holy Spirit of God, if he or she refuses to hate sin and evil and wrong, our churches might as well be turned into lodges or clubs.

O brother, sister! God has not given up loving us. The Holy Spirit still is God's faithful Spirit. Our Lord Jesus Christ is at the right hand of the Majesty in heaven, representing us there, interceding for us. God is asking us to stand in love and devotion to Him. The day is coming when judgment fire tries every person's work. The hay, wood and stubble of worldly achievement will be consumed. God wants us to know the reward of gold and silver and precious stones.

Following Jesus Christ is serious business. Let us quit being casual about heaven and hell and the judgment to come!

10

BE HOLY!

Just as he who called you is holy, so be holy in all you do; for it is written: "Be holy, because I am holy."

1 PETER 1:15–16

You cannot study the Bible diligently and earnestly without being struck by an obvious fact—the whole matter of personal holiness is highly important to God! Neither do you have to give long study to the attitudes of modern Christian believers to discern that, by and large, we consider the expression of true Christian holiness to be just a matter of personal option: "I have looked it over and considered it, but I don't buy it!"

I have always liked the word *exhort* better than *command*, so I remind you that Peter has given every Christian a forceful exhortation to holiness of life and conversation. He clearly bases this exhortation on two great facts—first, the character of God, and second, the command of God.

His argument comes out so simply that we sophisticates stumble over it—God's children ought to be holy because God

Himself is holy! We so easily overlook the fact that Peter was an apostle and he is here confronting us with the force of an apostolic injunction, completely in line with the Old Testament truth concerning the person and character of God and also in line with what the Lord Jesus had taught and revealed to His disciples and followers.

Personally, I am of the opinion that we who claim to be apostolic Christians do not have the privilege of ignoring such apostolic injunctions. I do not mean that a pastor can forbid or that a church can compel. I mean only that morally we dare not ignore this commandment: "Be ye holy."

Because it is an apostolic word, we must face up to the fact that we will have to deal with it in some way, and not ignore it—as some Christians do.

Certainly no one has provided us with an option in this matter. Who has ever given us the right or the privilege to look into the Bible and say, "I am willing to consider this matter and if I like it, I will buy it"—using the language of the day.

There is something basically wrong with our Christianity and our spirituality if we can carelessly presume that if we do not like a biblical doctrine and choose not to "buy" it, there is no harm done.

Commandments that we have received from our Lord or from the apostles cannot be overlooked or ignored by earnest and committed Christians. God has never instructed us that we should weigh His desires for us and His commandments to us in the balances of our own judgment and then decide what we want to do about them.

YOUR CHOICE

A professing Christian may say, "I have found a place of real Christian freedom; these things just don't apply to me." Of course you can walk out on it! God has given every one of us the power to make our own choices. I am not saying that we are forced to bow our necks to this yoke and we do not have to apply it to ourselves. It is true that if we do not like it, we can turn our backs on it.

The record in the New Testament is plain on this point—many people followed Jesus for a while and then walked away from Him. Once, Jesus said to His disciples: "Except ye eat the flesh of the Son of man, and drink his blood, ye have no life in you." Many looked at one another and then walked away from Him. Jesus turned to those remaining and said, "Will ye also go away?" Peter gave the answer which is still my answer today: "Lord, to whom shall we go? thou hast the words of eternal life" (John 6:53–68).

Those were wise words, indeed, words born of love and devotion.

So, we are not forced to obey in the Christian life, but we are forced to make a choice at many points in our spiritual maturity.

We have that power within us to reject God's instructions—but where else shall we go? If we refuse His words, which way will we turn? If we turn away from the authority of God's Word, to whose authority do we yield? Our mistake is that we generally turn to some other human—a man with breath in his nostrils.

WHAT HOLINESS IS

I am old-fashioned about the Word of God and its authority. I am committed to believe that if we ignore it or consider this commandment optional, we jeopardize our souls and earn for ourselves severe judgment to come.

Now, brethren, I have said that the matter of holiness is highly important to God. I have personally counted in an exhaustive concordance and found that the word *holiness* occurs 650 times in the Bible. I have not counted words with a similar meaning in English, such as *sanctify* and *sanctified*, so the count would jump nearer to a thousand if we counted these other words with the same meaning.

This word *holy* is used to describe the character of angels, the nature of heaven and the character of God. It is written that angels are holy and those angels who gaze down upon the scenes of mankind are called the watchers and holy ones.

It is said that heaven is a holy place where no unclean thing can enter in. God Himself is described by the adjective *holy*—Holy Ghost, Holy Lord and Holy Lord God Almighty. These words are used of God throughout the Bible, showing that the highest adjective that can be ascribed to God, the highest attribute that can be ascribed to God is that of holiness, and, in a relative sense, even the angels in heaven partake of the holiness of God.

We note in the Bible, too, that the absence of holiness is given as a reason for not seeing God. I am aware of some of the grotesque interpretations that have been given to the text: "holiness, without which no man shall see the Lord" (Heb. 12:14).

My position is this: I will not throw out this Bible text just because some people have misused it to support their own patented theory about holiness. This text does have a meaning and it ought to disturb us until we have discovered what it means and how we may meet its conditions.

What does this word *holiness* really mean? Is it a negative kind of piety from which so many people have shied away? No, of course not! Holiness in the Bible means moral wholeness—a positive quality which actually includes kindness, mercy, purity, moral blamelessness and godliness. It is always to be thought of in a positive, white intensity of degree.

Whenever it is written that God is holy, it means that God is kind, merciful, pure, and blameless in a white, holy intensity of degree. When used of men, it does not mean absolute holiness as it does of God, but it is still the positive intensity of the degree of holiness—and not negative.

This is why true Bible holiness is positive—a holy man can be trusted. A holy man can be tested. People who try to live by a negative standard of piety, a formula that has been copyrighted by other humans, will find that their piety does not stand up in times of difficult testing. Genuine holiness can be put into the place of testing without fear. Whenever there is a breakdown of holiness, that is proof there never was any real degree of holiness in the first place.

Personally, I truly have been affected in my heart by reading the testimonies and commentaries of humble men of God whom I consider to be among the great souls of Christian church history.

I have learned from them that the word and idea of holiness

as originally used in the Hebrew did not have first of all the moral connotation. It did not mean that God first of all was pure, for that was taken for granted! The original root of the word *holy* was of something beyond, something strange and mysterious and awe-inspiring. When we consider the holiness of God we talk about something heavenly, full of awe, mysterious, and fear-inspiring. Now, this is supreme when it relates to God, but it is also marked in men of God and deepens as men become more like God. It is a sense of awareness of the other world, a mysterious quality and difference that has come to rest upon some men—that is a holiness.

PURSUING HOLINESS

Now, if a man should have that sense and not be morally right, then I would say that he is experiencing a counterfeit of the devil. Whenever Satan has reason to fear a truth very gravely, he produces a counterfeit. He will try to put that truth in such a bad light that the very persons who are most eager to obey it are frightened away from it. Satan is very sly and very experienced in the forming of parodies of truth which he fears the most, and then pawns his parody off as the real thing and soon frightens away the serious-minded saints.

I regret to say that some who have called themselves by a kind of copyrighted name of holiness have allowed the doctrine to harden into a formula that has become a hindrance to repentance, for this doctrine has been invoked to cover up frivolity and covetousness, pride and worldliness. I have seen the results. Serious, honest persons have turned away from the whole idea of holiness because of those who have claimed it and then lived selfish and conceited lives.

But, brethren, we are still under the holy authority of the apostolic command. Men of God have reminded us in the Word that God does ask us and expect us to be holy men and women of God, because we are the children of God, who is holy. The doctrine of holiness may have been badly and often wounded—but the provision of God by His pure and gentle and loving Spirit is still the positive answer for those who hunger and thirst for the life and spirit well-pleasing to God.

When a good man with this special quality and mysterious Presence is morally right and walking in all the holy ways of God and carries upon himself without even knowing it the fragrance of a kingdom that is supreme above the kingdoms of this world, I am ready to accept that as being of God and from God!

SEEING HOLINESS

By way of illustration, remember that Moses possessed these marks and qualities when he came down from the mount. He had been there with God forty days and forty nights—and when he came back, everyone could tell where he had been. The lightning still played over his countenance, the glory of the Presence remained. This strange something which men cannot pin down or identify was there.

I lament that this mysterious quality of holy Presence has all but forsaken the earth in our day. Theologians long ago referred to it as the numinous, meaning that overplus of something that is more than righteous, but is righteous in a fearful, awe-inspiring, wondrous, heavenly sense. It is as though it is marked with a brightness, glowing with a mysterious fire.

I have commented that this latter quality has all but forsaken the earth and I think the reason is very obvious. We are men who have reduced God to our own terms. In the context of the Christian church, we are now told to "gossip" the gospel and "sell" Jesus to people! We still talk about righteousness, but we are lacking in that bright quality, that numinous that is beyond description.

This mysterious fire was in the bush as you will remember from the Old Testament. A small fire does not frighten people unless it spreads and gets out of control. We are not afraid of fire in that sense, yet we read how Moses, kneeling beside a bush where a small fire burned, hid his face for he was afraid! He had met that mysterious quality. He was full of awe in that manifested Presence.

Later, alone in the mountain and at the sounding of a trumpet, Moses shook, and said, "I exceedingly fear and quake" (Heb. 12:21). We are drawn again and again to that Shekinah that was over Israel for it sums up wonderfully this holiness of God's Presence. There was the overhanging cloud by day, plainly visible. It was a mysterious cloud not made of water vapor, not casting a shadow anywhere, mysterious. As the light of day would begin to fade, that cloud began to turn incandescent and when the darkness had settled, it shone brightly like one vast light hanging over Israel. Every tent in that diamond-shaped encampment was fully lighted by the strange Shekinah that hung over it. No man had built that fire. No one added any fuel—no one stoked or controlled it. It was God bringing Himself within the confines of the human eye and shining down in His Presence over Israel.

I can imagine a mother taking her little child by the hand to walk through the encampment. I am sure she would kneel down and whisper to that little fellow: "I want to show you something wonderful. Look! Look at that!"

Probably the response would be: "What is it, Mama?"

Then she would reply in a hushed voice: "That is God—God is there! Our leader Moses saw that fire in the bush. Later, he saw that fire in the mountain. Since we left Egypt that fire of God has followed us and hovered over us all through these years."

"But how do you know it is God, Mama?"

"Because of the Presence in that fire, the mysterious Presence from another world."

This Shekinah, this Presence, had no particular connotation of morality for Israel—that was all taken for granted. It did hold the connotation and meaning of reverence and awe, the solemn and inspiring, different and wonderful and glorious—all of that was there as it was also in the temple.

Then it came down again at Pentecost—that same fire sitting upon each of them—and it rested upon them with an invisible visibility. If there had been cameras, I do not think those tongues of fire could have been photographed—but they were there. It was the sense of being in or surrounded by this holy element, and so strong was it that in Jerusalem when the Christians gathered on Solomon's porch, the people stood off from them as wolves will stand away from a bright camp fire. They looked on, but the Bible says "and of the rest durst no man join himself to them" (Acts 5:13).

Why? Were they held back by any prohibition or restriction?

No one had been warned not to come near these praying people, humble and harmless, clean and undefiled. But the crowd could not come. They could not rush in and trample the place down. They stood away from Solomon's porch because they had sensed a holy quality, a mysterious and holy Presence within this company of believers.

Later, when Paul wrote to the Corinthian Christians to explain the mysterious fullness of the Holy Spirit of God, he [basically] said: "Some of you, when you meet together and you hear and obey God, know there is such a sense of God's presence that the unbelievers fall on their faces and then go out and report that God is with you indeed."

Now, that kind of Presence emanates from God as all holiness emanates from God. If we are what we ought to be in Christ and by His Spirit, if the whole sum of our lives beginning with the inner life is becoming more Godlike and Christlike, I believe something of that divine and mysterious quality and Presence will be upon us.

I have met a few of God's saints who appeared to have this holy brightness upon them, but they did not know it because of their humility and gentleness of spirit. I do not hesitate to confess that my fellowship with them has meant more to me than all of the teaching I have ever received. I do stand deeply indebted to every Bible teacher I have had through the years, but they did little but instruct my head. The brethren I have known who had this strange and mysterious quality and awareness of God's Person and Presence instructed my heart.

Do we understand what a gracious thing it is to be able to say of a man, a brother in the Lord, "He is truly a man of God"? He doesn't have to tell us that, but he lives quietly and confidently day by day with the sense of this mysterious, awe-inspiring Presence that comes down on some people and means more than all the glib tongues in the world!

Actually, I am afraid of all the glib tongues. I am afraid of the man who can always flip open his Bible and answer every question—he knows too much! I am afraid of the man who has thought it all out and has a dozen epigrams he can quote, the answers which he has thought up over the years to settle everything spiritual. Brethren, I'm afraid of it! There is a silence that can be more eloquent than all human speech. Sometimes there is a confusion of face and bowing of the head that speaks more divine truth than the most eloquent preacher can impart.

BEING HOLY

So, Peter reminds us that it is the Lord who has said: "Be ye holy as I am holy, and because I am holy."

First, bring your life into line morally so that God can make it holy; then bring your spiritual life into line that God may settle upon you with the Holy Ghost—with that quality of the Wonderful and the Mysterious and the Divine.

You do not cultivate it and you do not even know it, but it is there and it is this quality of humility invaded by the Presence of God that the church of our day lacks. Oh, that we might yearn for the knowledge and Presence of God in our lives from moment to moment, so that without human cultivation and without toilsome seeking there would come upon us this enduement that gives meaning to our witness! It is a sweet and radiant fragrance and I suggest that in some of our churches it may be strongly sensed and felt.

Now that I have said that, I had better stop and predict that some will ask me, "You don't go by your feelings, do you, Mr. Tozer?" Well, I do not dismiss the matter of feeling and you can quote me on that if it is worth it! Feeling is an organ of knowledge and I do not hesitate to say so. Feeling is an organ of knowledge.

To develop this, will you define the word love for me? I don't believe you can actually define love—you can describe it but you cannot define it. A person or a group of people or a race that has never heard of the word love can never come to an understanding of what love is even if they could memorize the definitions in all of the world's dictionaries.

But just consider what happens to any simple, freckle-faced boy with his big ears and his red hair awry when he first falls in love and the feeling of it comes into every part of his being. All at once, he knows more about love than all of the dictionaries put together!

This is what I am saying—love can only be understood by the feeling of it. The same is true with the warmth of the sun. Tell a man who has no feeling that it is a warm day, and he will never understand what you mean. But take a normal man who is out in the warm sun, and he will soon know it is warm. You can know more about the sun by feeling than you can by description.

So there are qualities in God that can never be explained to the intellect and can only be known by the heart, the innermost being. That is why I say that I do believe in feeling. I believe in what the old writers called religious affection—and we have so little of it because we have not laid the groundwork for it. The groundwork is repentance and obedience and separation and holy living!

I am confident that whenever this groundwork is laid, there will come to us this sense of the other-worldly Presence of God and it will become wonderfully, wonderfully real.

I have at times heard an expression in our prayers, "Oh, God, draw feelingly near!"

I don't think that is too far off—in spite of those who can only draw back and sit in judgment.

"Oh, God, come feelingly near!" God drew feelingly near to Moses in the bush and on the mount. He came feelingly near to the church at Pentecost and He came feelingly near to that Corinthian church when the unbelievers went away awe-struck to report that "God is really in their midst!"

I am willing to confess in humility that we need this in our day.

THE IMPORTANCE OF DEEDS

Faith without deeds is useless.

JAMES 2:20

It would be a convenient arrangement were we so constituted that we could not talk better than we live. For reasons known to God, however, there seems to be no necessary connection between our speaking and our doing; and here lies one of the deadliest snares in the religious life. I am afraid we modern Christians are long on talk and short on conduct. We use the language of power, but our deeds are the deeds of weakness.

Our Lord and His apostles were long on deeds. The Gospels depict a Man walking in power, "who went about doing good, and healing all that were oppressed of the devil; for God was with him" (Acts 10:38). The moral relation between words and deeds appears quite plainly in the life and teachings of Christ; He did before He spoke and the doing gave validity to the speaking.

Luke wrote of "all that Jesus began both to do and teach"

(Acts 1:1), and I am sure that the order expressed there is not accidental. In the Sermon on the Mount Christ placed doing before teaching: "Whosoever therefore shall break one of these least commandments, and shall teach men so, he shall be called the least in the kingdom of heaven: but whosoever shall do and teach them, the same shall be called great in the kingdom of heaven" (Matt. 5:19).

WORDS ARE EASY

Since in one of its aspects religion contemplates the invisible, it is easy to understand how it can be erroneously made to contemplate the unreal. The praying man talks of that which he does not see, and fallen human minds tend to assume that what cannot be seen is not of any great importance, and probably not even real, if the truth were known. So religion is disengaged from practical life and retired to the airy region of fancy where dwell the sweet insubstantial nothings that everyone knows do not exist but that they nevertheless lack the courage to repudiate publicly.

I could wish that this were true only of pagan religions and of the vague and ill-defined quasi-religion of the average man; but candor dictates that I admit it to be true also of much that passes for evangelical Christianity in our times. Indeed, it is more than possible that the gods of the heathen are more real to them than is the God of the average Christian. I sympathize with the mood of the poet Wordsworth when he wrote to the effect that he would rather be a sincere pagan who believed in a god that did not exist than to be a sophisticated Christian who disbelieved in a God who did.

Unquestionably there is not another institution in the world that talks as much and does as little as the church. Any factory that required as much raw material for so small a finished product would go bankrupt in six months. I have often thought that if one-tenth of one percent of the prayers made in the churches of any ordinary American village on one Sunday were answered, the country would be transformed overnight. But that is just our trouble. We pour out millions of words and never notice that the prayers are not answered. I trust it may not be uncharitable to say that we not only do not expect our prayers to be answered but would be embarrassed or even disappointed if they were. I think it is not uncommon for Christians to present eloquent petitions to the Lord that they know will accomplish nothing, and some of those petitions they dare present only because they know that is the last they will hear of the whole thing. Many a wordy brother would withdraw his request quickly enough if he had any intimation that God was taking it seriously.

We settle for words in religion because deeds are too costly. It is easier to pray, "Lord, help me to carry my cross daily" than to pick up the cross and carry it; but since the mere request for help to do something we do not actually intend to do has a certain degree of religious comfort, we are content with repetition of the words.

The practice of substituting words for deeds is not something new. The apostle John saw symptoms of it in his day and warned against it: "My little children, let us not love in word, neither in tongue; but in deed and in truth. And hereby we know that we are of the truth, and shall assure our hearts before him" (1 John 3:18–19). James also had something to say about the vice of words without deeds: "If a brother or sister be naked, and destitute of daily food, and one of you say unto them, Depart in peace, be ye warmed and filled; notwithstanding ye give them not those things which are needful to the body; what doth it profit?" (James 2:15–16)

What then: Shall we take a vow of silence? Shall we cease to pray and sing and write and witness till we catch upon our deeds? No. That would not help. We Christians are left in the world to witness, and while we have breath we must speak to men about God and to God about men. How then shall we escape the snare of words without deeds?

It is simple, though not easy. First, let us say nothing we do not mean. Break the habit of conventional religious chatter. Speak only as we are ready to take the consequences. Believe God's promises and obey His commandments. Practice the truth and we may with propriety speak the truth. Deeds give body to words. As we do acts of power our words will take on authority and a new sense of reality will fill our hearts.

FAITH IN ACTION

The supreme purpose of the Christian religion is to make men like God in order that they may act like God. In Christ the verbs *to be* and *to do* follow each other in that order. True religion leads to moral action. The only true Christian is the practicing Christian. Such a one is in very reality an incarnation of Christ as Christ is the incarnation of God; not in the same degree and fullness of perfection, for there is nothing in the moral universe equal to that awful mystery of godliness that joined God and man in eternal union in the person of the Man Christ Jesus; but as the fullness of the Godhead was and is in Christ, so Christ is in the nature of the one who believes in Him in the manner prescribed in the Scriptures.

God always acts like Himself wherever He may be and whatever He may be doing. When God became flesh and dwelt among us He did not cease to act as He had been acting from eternity. "He veiled His deity but He did not void it." The ancient name dimmed down to spare the helpless eyes of mortal men, but as much as was seen was true fire. Christ restrained His powers but He did not violate His holiness. In whatsoever He did He was holy, harmless, separate from sinners and higher than the highest heaven.

Just as in eternity God acted like Himself and when incarnated in human flesh still continued in all His conduct to be true to His holiness, so does He when He enters the nature of a believing man. This is the method by which He makes the redeemed man holy. He enters a human nature at regeneration as He once entered human nature at the incarnation and acts as becomes God, using that nature as a medium of expression for His moral perfections.

Cicero, the Roman orator, once warned his hearers that they were in danger of making philosophy a substitute for action instead of allowing it to produce action. What is true of philosophy is true also of religion. The faith of Christ was never intended to be an end in itself nor to serve instead of something else. In the minds of some teachers faith stands in lieu of moral conduct and every inquirer after God must take his choice between the two. We are presented with the well-known either/

or: Either we have faith or we have works, and faith saves while works damn us. Hence the tremendous emphasis on faith and the apologetic, mincing approach to the doctrine of personal holiness in modern evangelism. This error has lowered the moral standards of the church and helped to lead us into the wilderness where we currently find ourselves.

Rightly understood, faith is not a substitute for moral conduct but a means toward it. The tree does not serve in lieu of fruit but as an agent by which fruit is secured. Fruit, not trees, is the end God has in mind in yonder orchard; so Christlike conduct is the end of Christian faith. To oppose faith to works is to make the fruit the enemy to the tree; yet that is exactly what we have managed to do. And the consequences have been disastrous.

A miscalculation in laying the foundation of a building will throw the whole superstructure out of plumb, and the error that gave us faith as a substitute for action instead of faith in action has raised up in our day unsymmetrical and ugly temples of which we may well be ashamed and for which we shall surely give a strict account in the day when Christ judges the secrets of our hearts.

In practice we may detect the subtle—and often unconscious—substitution when we hear a Christian assure someone that he will "pray over" his problem, knowing full well that he intends to use prayer as a substitute for service. It is much easier to pray that a poor friend's needs may be supplied than to supply them. James's words burn with irony: "If a brother or sister be naked, and destitute of daily food, and one of you say unto them, Depart in peace, be ye warmed and filled; notwithstanding ye give them not those things which are needful to the body; what doth it profit?" (James 2:15–16). And the mystical John sees also the incongruity involved in substituting religion for action: "But whoso hath this world's good, and seeth his brother have need, and shutteth up his bowels of compassion from him, how dwelleth the love of God in him? My little children, let us not love in word, neither in tongue; but in deed and in truth. And hereby we know that we are of the truth, and shall assure our hearts before him" (1 John 3:17–19).

A proper understanding of this whole thing will destroy the false and artificial either/or. Then we will have not less faith but more godly works; not less praying but more serving; not fewer words but more holy deeds; not weaker profession but more courageous possession; not a religion as a substitute for action but religion in faith-filled action.

And what is that but to say that we will have come again to the teaching of the New Testament?

12

PREPARING FOR HEAVEN

For he was looking forward to the city with foundations,
whose architect and builder is God.

HEBREWS 11:10

I have found there is an entirely new way to shock complacent Christians in our churches today. These Christians go into shock when I say that it is an error to assume that being saved is to be automatically ready for heaven. Very few people in our churches are willing to consider what the Bible actually teaches about discipline and chastening in preparing us for our heavenly home. The writer of the letter to the Hebrews gave definite instruction to those who were children of God through faith in our Lord Jesus Christ:

If ye endure chastening, God dealeth with you as with sons; for what son is he whom the father chasteneth not? But if ye be without chastisement, whereof all are partakers, then are ye bastards, and not sons. . . . He [chastens us] for our profit, that we might be partakers of his holiness. . . . Follow peace with all men, and holiness, without which no man shall see the Lord. (Heb. 12:7–14)

Now, I know I will have to explain what I mean about our daily Christian lives being in preparation for an eternity in the heavenly realms. First, let us see if we are in agreement about the most important proclamation we can make concerning faith.

There is no doubt about it. First in importance concerning faith is the good news—the truth that every man and woman in our lost world may have God's gifts of forgiveness and eternal life through believing faith in Jesus Christ as Savior and Lord. It is not possible to overstate the importance of this basic truth in the Christian gospel. It has been proclaimed often. Paul gave this stark, simple instruction concerning salvation to the jailer at Philippi: "Believe on the Lord Jesus Christ, and thou shalt be saved, and thy house" (Acts 16:31).

As Christian believers (I am assuming you are a believer), you and I know how we have been changed and regenerated and assured of eternal life by faith in Jesus Christ and His atoning death. On the other hand, where this good news of salvation by faith is not known, religion becomes an actual bondage. If Christianity is known only as a religious institution, it may well become merely a legalistic system of religion, and the hope of eternal life becomes a delusion.

GOD'S OBJECTIVE IS OUR HOLINESS

I have said this much about the reality and assurance of our salvation through Jesus Christ to counter the shock you may feel when I add that God wants to fully prepare you in your daily Christian life so that you will be ready indeed for heaven. Perhaps it is a good thing for you if you are shocked. It is my observation that many Christians are so cosmopolitan, so worldly wise, so self-assured that they are past being shocked by anything!

Probably your first question as you come out of shock will be, "Have you forgotten the dying thief? Did not our Lord tell him his faith had made him ready for paradise?"

Let me share something with you. No one could love the Christian gospel and witness it to others without an understanding that the God of all grace has surely made a necessary provision for those who may trust Jesus in the final hours of life. We admit our humanness. We do not have God's wisdom and discernment. Only God is all-knowing and all-powerful. He is full of grace and truth. We can trust Him to be faithful and right in all of His dealings with us.

Remember that most believers have been found of the Lord and received His love and grace at an earlier time in their lives. Many testify to faith extending back to their childhood. Thus, they have been in God's household for a long time, and He has been trying to do something special within their beings day after day, year after year. His purpose has been to bring many sons— and daughters, too—to glory.

Now, if we are truly sons and daughters by faith, we will respond to the wise discipline and the necessary rebukes aimed at bringing us to the full measure of spiritual stature. God's motives are loving. Our heavenly Father disciplines us for our own good, "that we might be partakers of his holiness" (Heb. 12:10).

I have known people who seemed to be terrified by God's loving desire that we should reflect His own holiness and goodness. As God's faithful children, we should be attracted to holiness, for holiness is God-likeness—likeness to God!

God encourages every Christian believer to follow after holiness. Holiness is to be our constant ambition—not as holy as God is holy, but holy because God is holy. We know who we are and God knows who He is. He does not ask us to be God, and He does not ask us to produce the holiness that only He Himself knows. Only God is holy absolutely; all other beings can be holy only in relative degrees.

The angels in heaven do not possess God's holiness. They are created beings and they are contented to reflect the glory of God. That is their holiness.

Holiness is not terrifying. Actually, it is amazing and wonderful that God should promise us the privilege of sharing in His nature. It is impossible for any person to be as holy as God is holy. It is encouraging that God "knoweth our frame" (Ps. 103:14). He remembers we were made of dust. So He tells us what is in His being as He thinks of us: "Be holy because I am your God and I am holy! It is My desire that you grow in grace and in the knowledge of Me. I want you to be more like Jesus, My eternal Son, every day you live!"

Our Lord endeavors to prepare us for our eternal fellowship with the saints, the martyrs, the heroes of the faith who suffered through fire and flood and blood and tears when they were

God's pilgrims on this earth. Do not try to short-circuit God's plans for your discipleship and spiritual maturing here. If you and I were already prepared for heaven in that moment of our conversion, God would have taken us there instantly!

As believers and disciples, we are satisfied to know that the mysterious quality of God's holy person sets Him apart from all others and all else throughout His entire universe. God exists in Himself. His holy nature is such that we cannot comprehend Him with our minds.

God's holy nature is unique. He is of a substance not shared by any other being. Hence, God can be known only as He reveals Himself. There is absolutely no other way for us to know Him.

TODAY WE MAY
ENJOY GOD'S PRESENCE

In Old Testament times, whenever this utterly holy God revealed Himself in some way to mankind, terror and amazement were the reaction. People saw themselves as guilty and unclean by contrast.

Early in the Revelation, the final book of the Bible, the apostle John describes the overwhelming nature of his encounter with the Lord of glory. He says, "And when I saw him, I fell at his feet as dead" (Rev. 1:17). John was a man, a person born into a sinful world. But he was a believer and an apostle. At the time, he was in exile "for the word of God, and for the testimony of Jesus Christ" (1:9). But when the risen, glorified Lord Jesus appeared to him on Patmos, John sank down in abject humility and fear.

Jesus at once reassured him, stooping to place a nail-pierced hand on the prostrate apostle. "Fear not," Jesus said to John. "I am the first and the last: I am he that liveth, and was dead; and, behold, I am alive for evermore, Amen; and have the keys of hell and of death" (1:17–18). Then Jesus proceeded to give His apostle a writing assignment: "Write the things which thou hast seen, and the things which are, and the things which shall be hereafter" (1:19).

I notice particularly that the Lord did not condemn John. He knew that John's weakness was the reaction to revealed divine strength. He knew that John's sense of unworthiness was the instant reaction to absolute holiness. Along with John, every redeemed human being needs the humility of spirit that can only be brought about by the manifest presence of God.

This mysterious yet gracious Presence is the air of life eternal. It is the music of existence, the poetry of the Christian life. It is the beauty and wonder of being one of Christ's own—a sinner born again, regenerated, created anew to bring glory to God. To know this Presence is the most desirable state imaginable for anyone. To live surrounded by this sense of God is not only beautiful and desirable, but it is also imperative!

Know that our living Lord is unspeakably pure. He is sinless, spotless, immaculate, stainless. In His person is an absolute fullness of purity that our words can never express. This fact alone changes our entire human and moral situation and outlook. We can always be sure of the most important of all positives: God is God and God is right. He is in control. Because He is God He will never change!

I repeat: God is right—always. That statement is the basis of all we are thinking about God.

HOLINESS TAKES TIME

When the eternal God Himself invites us to prepare ourselves to be with Him throughout the future ages, we can only bow in delight and gratitude, murmuring, "Oh, Lord, may Your will be done in this poor, unworthy life!"

I can only hope that you are wise enough, desirous enough and spiritual enough to face up to the truth that every day is another day of spiritual preparation, another day of testing and discipline with our heavenly destination in mind. For as I hope you have already seen, full qualification for eternity is not instant or automatic or painless.

I hope, too, that you may begin to understand in this context why our evangelical churches are in such a mess. It has become popular to preach a painless Christianity and automatic saintliness. It has become a part of our "instant" culture. "Just pour a little water on it, stir mildly, pick up a gospel tract, and you are on your Christian way."

Lo, we are told, this is Bible Christianity. *It is nothing of the sort!* To depend upon that kind of a formula is to experience only the outer fringe, the edge of what Christianity really is. We must be committed to all that it means to believe in the Lord Jesus Christ. There must be a new birth from above; otherwise we are in religious bondage and legalism and delusion—or worse! But when the wonder of regeneration has taken place in our lives, then comes the lifetime of preparation with the guidance of the Holy Spirit.

God has told us that heaven and the glories of the heavenly kingdom are more than humans can ever dream or imagine. It will be neither an exhibition of the commonplace nor a democracy for the spiritually mediocre.

Why should we try to be detractors of God's gracious and rewarding plan of discipleship? God has high plans for all of His redeemed ones. It is inherent in His infinite being that His motives are love and goodness. His plans for us come out of His eternal and creative wisdom and power. Beyond that is His knowledge and regard for the astonishing potential that lies resident in human nature, long asleep in sin but awakened by the Holy Spirit in regeneration.

Yes, God is preparing us by making us disciples of Christ. A disciple is one who is in training. Being a disciple of Christ brings us to the day-by-day realities of such terms as discipline, rebuke, correction, hardship. Those are not pleasant words. To be admonished and instructed, to be punished and reproved, to be trained and corrected—no one chooses these things because they are neither pleasant nor entertaining. But they are in God's plan for our spiritual maturity.

WHAT WILL BE OUR RESPONSE?

In times of testing and hardship, I have heard Christians cry in their discouragement, "How can I believe that God loves me?" The fact is, God loves us to such a degree that He will use every necessary means to mature us until we reach "unity of the faith" and attain "unto the measure of the stature of the fulness of Christ" (Eph. 4:13).

A critic may cringe and charge that God is breaking our spirits, that we will be worth nothing as a result, that we will wear only a sad, hang-dog look for eternity. Oh, no! That is not true. What God plans is to bring us into accord with the wisdom and power and holiness that flow eternally from His throne.

God's loving motive is to bring us into total harmony with Himself so that moral power and holy usefulness become ours in this world and in the world to come.

This has been a message from my heart about down-to-earth preparation that will result in readiness for heaven's joys. Let me therefore conclude with a simple, down-to-earth illustration— the example of a newborn baby brought suddenly into the confusion of our noisy world.

Is the little fellow "ready" for this world in which he must live? When the time of his birth neared, the doctor told the parents-to-be, "The baby is ready!" So, as the baby was born, it could have been said in the biological sense that he was "ready."

But what do you really think? You must know that the baby is not really ready at all! From the first little whack he gets to make him cry and get his breath right on for the next eighteen or twenty years, that baby and child and young man will need to learn much about his environment. He will need to mature day by day.

In the broader social and human sense, he is not ready for this world until years have passed and he has completed his formal education. So it is with the Christian believer who has confessed his or her faith in Jesus Christ. Oh, yes, he or she is forgiven and "saved." But is he, is she automatically prepared for heaven and all of the eternal glories above?

To say yes is to be ridiculous. You might as well say that you can pick up a newborn baby, prop him up in the chair of the nation's President or Prime Minister and whisper in his ear that he is ready to govern.

My mind returns frequently to some of the old Christian saints who often prayed in their faith, "O God, we know this world is only a dressing room for the heaven to come!" They were very close to the truth in their vision of what God has planned for His children.

In summary: Down here the orchestra merely rehearses; over there we will give the concert. Here, we ready our garments of righteousness; over there we will wear them at the wedding of the Lamb.

13

GO AND TELL

Go and make disciples of all nations.

Matthew 28:19

We have all heard at some time about persons who were supposed to be "secret" or "silent" Christians. I have heard men say we will be surprised when we get to heaven and find people there who were secret Christians but who never talked about it. It is my opinion, brethren, that the silent Christian has something wrong with him.

There is an abnormal psychology called manic depressive, where people just go into silence. They won't talk—they just sit quiet. They just shut up, and that's all. There is something wrong with the mind that doesn't want to talk. God gave you a mouth, and He meant for you to use it to express some of the wonders that generate inside your being.

When we come to God in Christ, and we give ourselves to Him, one of the first things we do is to say, "Abba, Father!" Someone describing the Quakers said they don't talk about their religion—they live it. Oh, how foolish can we get? The things that are closest to our hearts are the things we talk about, and if God is close to your heart, you will talk about Him!

Think of the old dowagers who sit around the canasta table and smoke cigarettes by the yard—they never bring up the subject of religion. If anyone says, "Why don't you talk about religion, or God, or faith?" they have a reply: "Oh, that's something too sacred to mention!" So, they excuse themselves on the grounds that some things are too sacred to talk about. Actually, there are some things they have never seen and can't describe—that's their trouble. There are some places they have never been—so they are on unfamiliar ground. That's their trouble.

Oh, this quiet religion that says: "I haven't anything to say . . . oh, no! I worship God in my heart."

No you don't, brother! The heavenly beings said with their voices, "Holy, holy, holy!"

The Bible links faith to expression, and faith that never gets expression is not a Bible faith. For we believe in our hearts, and utter forth with our lips that Jesus Christ is Lord, and we shall be saved. You say: "Well, I worship God in my heart." I wonder if you do. I wonder if you are simply just excusing the fact that you haven't generated enough spiritual heat to get your mouth open!

TELLING OTHERS

Spiritual experiences must be shared. It is not possible for very long to enjoy them alone. The very attempt to do so will destroy them.

The reason for this is obvious. The nearer our souls draw to

God, the larger our love will grow; and the greater our love, the more unselfish we shall become and the greater our care for the souls of others. Hence increased spiritual experience, so far as it is genuine, brings with it a strong desire that others may know the same grace that we ourselves enjoy. This leads quite naturally to an increased effort to lead others to a closer and more satisfying fellowship with God.

The human race is one. God "made of one blood all nations of men for to dwell on all the face of the earth," and He made the individual members of society for each other. Not the hermit but the man in the midst of society is in the place best to fulfill the purpose for which he was created. There may be circumstances when for a time it will be necessary for the seeker after God to wrestle alone like Jacob on the bank of the river, but the result of his lonely experience is sure to flow out to family and friend, and on out to society at last. In the nature of things it must be so.

The impulse to share, to impart, normally accompanies any true encounter with God and spiritual things. The woman at the well, after her soul-inspiring meeting with Jesus, left her waterpots, hurried into the city and tried to persuade her friends to come out and meet Him. "Come, see a man," she said, "which told me all things that ever I did: is not this the Christ?" Her spiritual excitement could not be contained within her own heart. She had to tell someone.

Is it not possible that our Lord had this in mind when He spoke about the impossibility of secret discipleship? Have we misunderstood the true relationship between faith and testimony? Christ made it clear that there could be no such thing as secret discipleship and Paul said, "With the heart man believeth unto righteousness; and with the mouth confession is made unto salvation." This is usually understood to mean that God has laid upon us an arbitrary requirement to open our mouth in confession before salvation can become effective within us. Maybe that is the correct meaning of these verses. Or could it be that the confession is an evidence of the salvation that has come by faith to the heart, and where there is no impulse to impart, no outrushing of words in joyous testimony, there has been no true inward experience of saving grace?

The irrepressible urge to share spiritual blessings can explain a great many religious phenomena. It even goes so far as to create a kind of vicarious transfer of interest from one person to another, so that the blessed soul would if necessary give up its own blessing that another might receive. Only thus can that prayer of Moses be understood, "Oh, this people have sinned a great sin, and have made them gods of gold. Yet now, if thou wilt forgive their sin—; and if not, blot me, I pray thee, out of thy book which thou hast written" (Exod. 32:31–32). His great care for Israel had made him incautious, almost rash, before the Lord in their behalf. Moses felt that for Israel to be forgiven was reward enough for him. This impulsive uprush of vicarious love can hardly be defended before the bar of pure reason. But God understood and complied with Moses's request.

The intense urge to have others enjoy the same spiritual privileges as himself once led Paul to make a statement so extreme, so reckless, that reason cannot approve it; only love can understand: "I say the truth in Christ, I lie not, my conscience also bearing me witness in the Holy Ghost, that I have great heaviness and continual sorrow in my heart. For I could wish that myself were accursed from Christ for my brethren, my kinsmen according to the flesh" (Rom. 9:1–3).

In the light of this it is quite easy to understand why all great Christian teachers have insisted that true spiritual experience must be shared. The careless person who remarks that he does not need to go to church to serve God is far from understanding the most elementary spiritual truths. By cutting himself off from the religious community he proves that he has never felt the deep urge to share—and for the very reason that he has nothing to share. He has never felt the constraining love of Christ, so he can go his way in silence. His withdrawal from the believing fellowship tells us more about him than he knows about himself.

"Being let go, they went to their own company."

So it was in the early church and so it has always been when men meet God in saving encounter. They want to share the blessed benefits.

REFERENCES

Chapter 1: Marks of Discipleship
The Set of the Sail (Camp Hill, PA: Christian Publications, 1990; repr. Chicago: WingSpread Publishers, 2009), 137–44.

Chapter 2: True and False Disciples
Faith Beyond Reason (Camp Hill, PA: Christian Publications, 1990; repr. Camp Hill, PA: WingSpread Publishers, 2009), 51–68.

Chapter 3: "Accepting" Christ
Christ the Eternal Son (Camp Hill, PA: Christian Publications, 1982; repr. Chicago: WingSpread Publishers, 2010), 144–61.

Chapter 4: To All Who Received Him
Faith Beyond Reason, 1–13.

Chapter 5: Obedience Is Not an Option
I Call It Heresy (Camp Hill, PA: Christian Publications, 1991; repr. Camp Hill, PA: WingSpread Publishers, 2010), 1–13.

Chapter 6: You Cannot Face Two Directions

Tozer Speaks, Volume 1 (Camp Hill, PA: Christian Publications, 1994; repr. Camp Hill, PA: WingSpread Publishers, 2010), 259–73.

Chapter 7: Crucified with Christ
Tozer Speaks, Volume 2 (Camp Hill, PA: Christian Publications, 1994; repr. Camp Hill, PA: WingSpread Publishers, 2010), 294–303, 304–12.

Chapter 8: Take Up Your Cross
The Radical Cross (Camp Hill, PA: Christian Publications, 2005; repr. Chicago: Moody Publishers, 2015), 153–56, 67–69.

Chapter 9: Loving Righteousness, Hating Evil
Jesus, Our Man in Glory (Camp Hill, PA: Christian Publications, 1987; repr. Chicago: WingSpread Publishers, 2009), 59–70.

Chapter 10: Be Holy!
Tozer Speaks, Volume 2, 57–69.

Chapter 11: The Importance of Deeds
Born After Midnight (Camp Hill, PA: Christian Publications, 1959; repr. Chicago: Moody Publishers, 2015), 39–43; *Of God and Men* (Camp Hill, PA: Christian Publications, 1960; repr. Chicago: Moody Publishers, 2015), 67–70.

Chapter 12: Preparing for Heaven

Jesus, Author of Our Faith (Camp Hill, PA: Christian Publications, 1988; repr. Camp Hill, PA: WingSpread Publishers, 2007), 88–98.

Chapter 13: Go and Tell
Tozer Speaks, Volume 1, 24–25; *The Set of the Sail*, 50–53.

ENCOUNTER GOD. WORSHIP MORE.

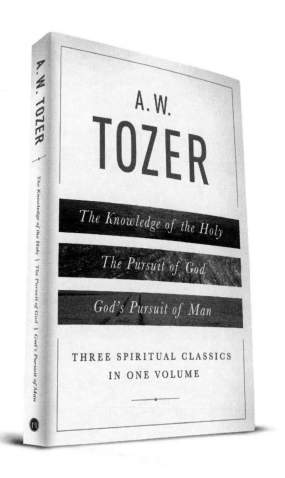

MOODY
Publishers®

From the Word to Life®

Considered to be Tozer's greatest works, *The Knowledge of the Holy*, *The Pursuit of God*, and *God's Pursuit of Man* are now available in a single volume. In *Three Spiritual Classics*, you will discover a God of breathtaking majesty and world-changing love, and you will find yourself worshipping through every page.

978-0-8024-1861-6

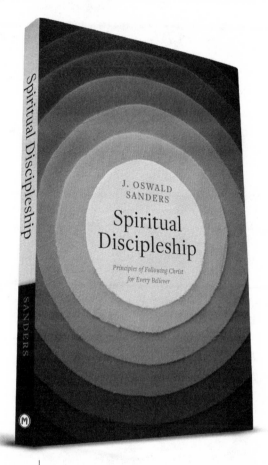

COMPLETE THE COLLECTION

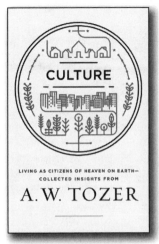

ISBN 978-1-60066-801-2

ISBN 978-0-8024-1520-2

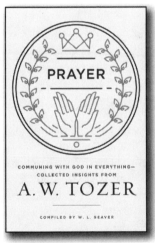

ISBN 978-0-8024-1381-9

ISBN 978-0-8024-1603-2

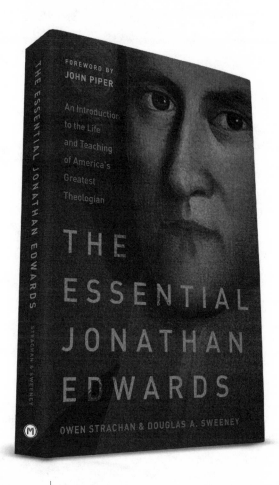